ZIMBABWE SAFARI

A Memoir by Tim Good

Laughing Hyena Press   Tucson, Arizona

Copyright © 2020 by Timothy R. Good

All rights reserved. No part of this book may be reproduced or transmitted in any form or by any means, electronic or mechanical, including photocopying, recording, or by any information storage and retrieval system, without permission in writing from the author.

This edition was prepared for publication by
Ghost River Images
5350 East Fourth Street
Tucson, Arizona 85711
www.ghostriverimages.com

To communicate with the author
contact us at
buffalo_tim@me.com

Cover design by
Tim Good

ISBN: 978-1-7347951-1-0

Library of Congress Control Number: 2020911378

Published in the United States of America

Second Print Edition: July, 2020

Contents

Preface	7
Acknowledgments	9
The Dream	11
Starting the Adventure	17
Getting There	23
Arriving in Zimbabwe	27
Leopard	43
Cape Buffalo	55
Elephant	69
Other Hunts	83

    Impala, Hyena, Rogue Elephant, Greater Kudu, Nyala, Bushbuck, The Tiny Ten, Eland, Jackal, Warthog, Waterbuck, Zebra

Other Species	111

    Lion, Baboon, Crocodile, Hippopotamus, Cheetah, Wild Dogs, Fishing, Egyptian Geese, Vultures, Red-billed Quelea, Guineafowl, Secretary Bird, Martial Eagle, Yellow-billed Hornbill

Other Stories	127

    My Taxidermist, Public Transportation in the Bush, Matobo National Park, Chipangali Wildlife Orphanage, Russian Hunters, The Great Zimbabwe, Elephant Stories, Bubi River Hotel & Bar, Poaching, Malaria

End of the Hunt	143
Hank's Lion: a short story	147
Appendix A	159

    My Opinion: Hunting Ethics

Appendix B	161

    Elk Hunting in Utah, Wolf Hunting in Wyoming, Bison Hunting in Colorado

Appendix C	169

    The Thornton Boys

Preface

Every passion has its Holy Land.

Oil painters go to The Louvre
Tennis players go to Wimbledon
Golfers go to St Andrews
Hunters go to Africa

I have greatly enjoyed my hunting trips to Africa. I've seen things I only dreamed of seeing. I've followed the footsteps of the great explorers of Africa.

After several trips and watching the winds of time, I believe that African hunting might be moving towards the of its line.

I had a fantasy of hunting in Africa with my family. I know that won't happen. By the time my great-grandchildren will be able to hunt, I am afraid that, despite current conservation efforts, hunting in Africa won't exist.

I hope this memoir goes some distance towards answering that obvious question from my descendants: "Great-Grandpa hunted? In Africa? Why?"

Well, great-grandchild, your Great-Grandpa was an American hunter. And here's why…

8

Acknowledgments

I've had much help and guidance creating the written memories of my African adventures.

Chap Esterhuizen, Thabani (Tubbs) Ncube and Japhet Chuma... who led me to my adventures in Africa, and taught me what I know.

Jack Thornton... who gave me guidance on writing, grammar, sentence structure, and is a Hemingway *aficionado*.

The Tucson Writing Guild... including Cortney Webb, David Piatt, Rene Miranda, Dov Miklofsky, Greg Duke...who provided guidance, encouragement and proofing.

Exercise partners: Siri-Dya Khalsa & Doug Miller... They kept me going!

Jessica Ashby... my "Idea Reader", who gave me important structure thoughts.

John Geary and Mark Meyer... proofread my work.

Mike White of Ghost River Images... helped me through the hard part.

Mike, Miranda, Kim, JoAnne, Nate-Dog, Sadie-Cat, Asher-Bear, Tex.

And, of course, Linda.

Graphics by JoAnne Meeker

Unwritten law of big game hunting:

You must be willing to shoot yourself out of whatever trouble you shot yourself into!

Christopher Ondaatje
Hemingway in Africa

The Dream

Although it wasn't hot, the equatorial sun beat down on us as we snaked through the underbrush in Zimbabwe's teak forest. After six hours of tracking, we slowly closed in on the huge bull elephant. I was being guided on this elephant hunt by a black African and a white African. I could barely make out the elephant in the dense green and yellow foliage, occasionally catching a glimpse of his well-camouflaged gray shape, which seemed to shift as he snapped branches off the surrounding trees and shoved them into his mouth. We had to be careful that the ancient beast didn't smell us, hear us, or see us. If he did, he would either explode away, making our tracking fruitless, or he would charge us with evil intent.

When we were within thirty yards, our tracker, Thabani, silently slipped to the rear of our hunting party, unnerving me. It was time for the final act of this hunt. Chap, carrying his heavy double rifle, slowly guided me closer, positioning me for a frontal brain shot, the most coveted by experienced elephant hunters. And the most dangerous.

I had to execute the shot perfectly. To fail would endanger the entire hunting party. However, this is exactly the situation I had wanted to be in since I was thirteen years old: in Africa, hunting an elephant.

• • •

I remember when I first became infatuated with Africa. It was in the early 1960s. My father, a career United States Air Force officer, was assigned to Ramstein Air Force Base in Germany. I don't remember why, but at thirteen years old I became interested in rifle shooting, so my father and I joined Ramstein's Rod and Gun Club. My father bought me an excellent .22 caliber target rifle, and I began shooting with the junior Rod and Gun Club team. While my father didn't hunt, he enjoyed shooting. He was especially proud of continually qualifying "expert" with a Colt M1911 .45 pistol.

Even with the targets as close as ten yards, I was a pretty good shot with my rifle. My intention was to hit the "ten ring," or bullseye, with the first shot and have subsequent rounds go through the same hole. I was actually able to accomplish this feat. Sometimes.

On one occasion, my father and I were walking past the Rod and Gun Club's outdoor range when we heard a tremendous explosion. Naturally, we went to see what had caused the commotion.

A young officer was holding an enormous rifle. As we drew closer, he fired downrange again, causing another tremendous explosion. As the young man put the rifle down, my father and I walked over to examine it.

"It's a .470 nitro express double rifle," he told us.

"What on earth do you use it for?"

"Hunting. In Africa," he said.

My God, I thought. His bullets dwarfed my .22 LR rounds. The .470 rounds were the size of my father's fingers.

"What do you hunt in Africa?"

"Elephant!"

That was it. I was hooked!

Throughout the years, because of family and professional reasons, I was never able to go to Africa, but I studied Africa.

Prince Henry the Navigator, third in line to the Portuguese throne, developed fifteenth-century sailing innovations that allowed ships to circumnavigate Africa, expanding the range of European exploration and trade.

Dutchman Jan van Riebeeck established Cape Town in 1652 in what is now South Africa. As a way station for the Dutch East India Company, Cape Town became the first permanent European settlement in southern Africa.

John Hanning Speke and Richard Francis Burton were English army officers serving the British military in India who went to Africa on furlough in the mid-1850s. Supported by the Royal Geographical Society, they were the first to explore the great lakes of Africa. Their goal, to find the source of the Nile, has been widely documented in books and film.

In the 1870s, Frederick Selous, an English explorer, hunter, soldier, and conservationist, explored the area in East Africa which became

Tanzania. Selous was the model for Allan Quatermain, the adventurer in H. Rider Haggard's 1885 novel *King Solomon's Mines*.

Perhaps the best known European to make an early mark on Africa was David Livingstone, Scottish doctor and missionary. Livingstone is famous for geographical discoveries (Victoria Falls, 1855), introducing God and Western medicine to the indigenous tribes of central Africa, fighting slavery, and being lost to the West and found by Henry Stanley, who greeted Livingstone with the famous, "Dr. Livingstone, I presume."

King Leopold II of Belgium established the Congo Free State in 1885 as a personal colony; his goal was to extract as much money for himself as possible from the region. The terrible treatment of the Congo basin people was well documented in Joseph Conrad's *Heart of Darkness*. In 1908, Belgium took control of the area, renaming it the Belgium Congo. When King Leopold II died in 1909, there was not an effective government in an area known as the Lado Enclave, located on the west bank of the Upper Nile in central Africa. The enclave became lawless. As this area held the last of the huge elephant herds, with old bulls carrying two hundred pounds of ivory, scores of Western elephant poachers flooded into the area. These scoundrels included John Boyes, two brothers named Craven, an old Scotsman named McQueen, James Manley, F.H. Clarke, and the most well-known, W.D.M. (Karamojo) Bell. These men, and others, shot thousands of elephants for their ivory. Many of these immoral poachers died, however, from Blackwater fever, an often fatal form of malaria.

After several years, sanity prevailed, and law and order came to the Lado Enclave. The poachers were expelled, although by that time vast herds of elephants had been killed.

East African settlers, mostly English, tried to turn the harsh British East African savanna and its inhospitable animals into a gentle English countryside. Hugh Cholmondeley, 3rd Baron Delamere, spent his family fortune in the early twentieth century developing farms and ranches in the wilderness of Kenya. Bror von Blixen and his wife, Karen, from Sweden, farmed coffee in Kenya with mixed success. Bror became an early professional hunter, as did his wife's lover, Dennis Finch Hatton.

By the early twentieth century, the first professional hunters were taking their clients on six- to nine-month safaris in East Africa. This line of work was started by English adventurers, some of the earliest being Richard Cunninghame (who guided Theodore Roosevelt on his African safari), Philip Percival (who guided Ernest Hemingway), and Harry Selby (who guided Robert Ruark).

I absorbed the African fiction and non-fiction of Hemingway, Hanley, and Ruark. I dreamed of adventure while watching movies: *The Snows of Kilimanjaro*, *The African Queen*, *Out of Africa*, and all three versions of *King Solomon's Mines*.

I read detailed accounts of the exploration of the great African rivers: the Nile, the Congo, and the Zambezi.

In zoos across America, Europe, and Asia, I saw big cats and bigger elephants, all trapped in steel enclosures. I dreamed of seeing a lion resting in the shade of a mopane tree next to a half-eaten zebra and watching a herd of elephants snapping acacia tree branches to eat as they wandered across the savanna.

Starting the Adventure

Somewhere in the transition from childhood to adulthood I determined I *must* hunt in Africa. Eventually, the time came.

I then had two big decisions to make: which animals I wanted to hunt and where in Africa I wanted to go.

In Africa there are two main categories of animals available to hunters: dangerous game and plains game. I knew I wanted to hunt dangerous game, which includes the Big Five: elephant, rhino, lion, leopard, and Cape buffalo. Plains game are the prey animals of Africa's carnivores and tend to resemble American deer, elk, and moose. The most commonly hunted plains animals include greater kudu, waterbuck, eland, bushbuck, and nyala.

I would have liked to hunt in Kenya. It was the location for African hunting in the classic literature I had read, but the country banned all hunting in 1976. I never considered any of the central African countries because I didn't want to hunt in swamps or jungles. The southern region of Africa, however, was a good option. It had an abundance of plains animals, and it had the Big Five. Rhino tags, however, were not available, as they had become endangered by my time.

Ultimately, I chose Zimbabwe (formally known as Rhodesia) in southern Africa. I had read about Cecil Rhodes' early exploits in southern Africa and the South African diamond mines and had become interested in traveling there. Specifically, I chose the Zambezi River Valley in northern Zimbabwe. The valley is a spectacular escarpment that was formed by the Zambezi River as it flowed down from Victoria Falls. Research on Zimbabwe hunting outfitters led me to Martin Pieters Safaris, and they connected me with professional hunter Chap Esterhuizen.

Just like in the United States, African countries have quotas on animals that can be hunted. In Zimbabwe, the quota for a species is determined within individual concessions of land. The hunting concessions are normally between 200,000-300,000 acres but can be larger.

A concession is normally allocated to one professional hunter and his client at a time, which is one reason why booking hunts in Africa can be a difficult task. Normally, the number of animals that can be hunted in these concessions is very small. Hunting a lion or elephant may require booking the hunt several years in advance. Endangered animals, such as the rhino, cheetah, and black-faced impala cannot be hunted at all.

I was going to Zimbabwe to hunt dangerous game, including Cape buffalo, leopard, and elephant, as well as any available plains game. With this decision in mind, I then had to decide what rifle I would use on the hunt. This was an important decision. Most African countries have a legal minimum caliber of .375 that can be used to hunt dangerous game. There are bigger rifles available, but the advantage of the .375 is that it can be used for smaller game as well, so I chose a bolt-action Winchester .375 Holland and Holland.

Although I could have used the iron sights on the rifle, I selected a detachable scope. A detachable scope allowed me to take the scope off the rifle during transport from America. The rifle case was strong, but I felt better taking the scope and my binoculars with me as carry-ons in the aircraft cabin. This ensured that my optics wouldn't get broken when some strong-bodied, weak-minded individual threw my rifle case across the tarmac.

I chose a scope with a range of 1x to 4x. On the 4x setting, if an animal was two hundred feet away, it would look like it was fifty feet away. This was only for longer-range shots, which in southern Africa would be seventy-five or one hundred yards. If I was in a situation with a dangerous animal within twenty yards, the scope would be set at natural eyesight, 1x, so that the distance wasn't misrepresented.

As for the ammunition, there are two types of bullets used on these hunts: solid and expanding. Solid bullets stay together upon impact and will drive through big, tough animals like elephant and Cape buffalo. Expanding bullets "flower," or expand, upon contact with the smaller, softer animals and cause extensive internal damage, ensuring a rapid death. Since I was going to hunt large, heavy animals as well as the smaller, more fragile animals, I had to take both.

I knew that I needed to practice my shooting before I went. I was not a great shot, but I believed I would improve with consistent practice.

I started going to the local rifle range on a regular basis, taking about ten bullets for the .375 with me each time. Eventually I got to the point where I could get most of the rounds inside the nine ring, hoping that this would be good enough.

As I improved my gunmanship, I began to build the collection of what I would take on the trip. Since many African countries do not allow camouflage, khaki is the most common color of African hunting clothes. I got two pairs of khaki pants, two pairs of khaki shorts, two long-sleeved khaki shirts, and two short-sleeved khaki shirts. I also added a fleece jacket for chilly evenings. For my footwear, I had sneakers for campsite use, flip flops for the shower, and specialized boots for hunting. The boots were the most important part of the kit. My boots were ankle high, rubber soled, and had leather tops that protected me from the infamous African thorns. They were not cheap, but this was not an area where I would save money. I needed the best quality boots I could buy. The last clothing additions to my hunting kit were gators—canvas attachments that fit over my boots to keep seeds and bugs out, several pairs of socks, and a hat. In terms of non-clothing items for my hunting kit, I included a sharp pocketknife, flashlight, rifle-cleaning kit, camera, batteries, and power cords with appropriate power plugs.

Chap encouraged me to wear my hunting clothes, especially my boots, on the flight to Africa. This was so if my luggage was lost, at least I would have the appropriate clothes with me. If my rifle and ammunition didn't show up, Chap could provide me with replacements. He could not, however, supply me with hunting boots or clothes that fit properly.

The final thing I needed to do to prepare for the trip was get in adequate physical shape. Hunting in Africa requires the ability to endure the long stalking hikes over hills and through valleys under the equatorial sun. Being a gentleman of some years, my physical condition prior to the hunt would not do. I had to improve it. I devised a three-part regimen to get into "hunting" shape.

First, I worked out at a gym with a personal trainer, Siri-Dya Khalsa, three days a week. S.D. knew my goals, so he gave me guidance to strengthen my body, focusing on my legs, core, and shoulders. Second, I met with a tennis professional, Doug Miller, three days a week and rallied around the court back and forth with him. This was the cardio component of my regimen. It gave me the endurance I needed to thrive during my multi-mile hunts over difficult terrain. Lastly, twice a week I carried my rifle and a backpack filled with rocks and water and went out into the Arizona desert for a two- or three-hour hike. This was the psychological training I needed to prepare myself to walk the long distances I would be covering in Africa.

While I knew that there would be many things outside my control on the hunt, my physical condition would not be one of them. At the end of the trail, I'd face an elephant, Cape buffalo, or leopard; I did not want my physical condition to be the cause of a disaster.

Getting There

Getting to Africa today is relatively easy compared to when client trophy hunting in Africa started early in the twentieth century. In the early years of African hunting, there were no passenger planes that flew from America to Africa. Travel to Africa was by sea.

In the 1920s, when rich Americans became aware of African hunting, they would frequently combine an African safari with business trips to London or Paris. They would sail from New York to Europe by luxury liner. The American hunters would complete their work in Europe, then continue to Africa.

However, the vessels going from Europe to Africa were not luxury liners. They were tramp steamers with room for a few passengers. The final leg of the journey to Africa usually started in Marseille, in southern France, and would stop numerous times en route to eastern Africa. The American hunter's only entertainment was walking the decks and reading, with shore excursions at the various small commercial ports.

The total sea route from New York to Africa included sailing through the Suez Canal and down the East African coast to the seaport of British East Africa, Mombasa, and it took weeks or months. Jet lag? Not at all.

Today, however, the Zambezi Valley hunter flies to New York, then to Johannesburg, South Africa, then to Victoria Falls, Zimbabwe, taking about twenty-eight hours. Convenient? Yes. Jet lag? Absolutely. Jet lag had to be addressed.

To start the process of traveling to Africa, I contacted an African travel specialist. The advantage of an African travel specialist was that he or she will have access to current visa, rifle, and ammunition processes, as well as knowing all the documents to provide. After coordinating the dates with my professional hunter, I had to arrange the flights. While flying to Africa, you should always leave two to three hours between flights, particularly at your first African destination. There are many flight delay opportunities when flying from Tucson to Zimbabwe.

Leaving America with a rifle is not easy, but arriving in your final destination with a rifle is *really* not easy. Zimbabwe customs require rifle serial number, description (caliber, manufacturer), and an ammunition count with the bullets in new, unopened boxes. The customs agent at the destination will open the boxes and count the rounds. The agents will take one copy of the form and leave you with two copies. When you finally leave Zimbabwe, you will go through the same process, in reverse, leaving the second copy with the agent. Assuming all the counts and serial numbers match, you may now enter the country of Zimbabwe with your gear.

As of this writing, Zimbabwe is a safe country for the client hunter. Zimbabwe is a very poor country, and all Zimbabweans appreciate the influx of Western hunters' dollars. The only danger to hunters is from the Big Five, crocodile, hyena, hippo, poisonous snakes, and malaria. Malaria is the only serious disease to be caught in Zimbabwe, but it's easily avoided if you take your anti-malarial pills without failure. And you must take malaria pills.

Arriving in Zimbabwe

Chap, a native Zimbabwean, was my professional hunter. He grew up in Bulawayo, a major city in Zimbabwe, and he hunted the area with his father throughout his youth. During school, he decided to become a professional hunter.

He eventually received his license to lead clients on dangerous game hunts, but this was not an easy process. He had to pass field tests, know the scientific names of all plants and animals in Zimbabwe, and hunt game, including dangerous game, under the watchful eye of professional hunters. Then he had to serve several years as an apprentice at a hunting camp doing shit tasks, including building and repairing hunting camps and roads. He also occasionally had to help with hunting problems, such as locating and sorting out (tracking down and killing) wounded animals.

As an apprentice, Chap had the opportunity to hunt with the late Mark Ellement, a noted elephant hunter, and John Sharp, a professional hunter famous for looking like a professional hunter. Because of this, Chap is partial to elephant hunting. And he looks good doing it.

Chap is a very skilled professional hunter—knowledgeable, brave, and a great shot with large caliber rifles. He is six feet tall, sturdy with endless strength and endurance. Chap speaks both Ndebele and Shona, the two tribal languages of Zimbabwe. He's very personable with his clients, and he's a great manager of his staff, which includes Thabani (Tubbs) Ncube, a lifelong tracker, and Japhet Chuma, a skilled tracker who also serves as Chap's driver and mechanic.

Chap is also known for the hunting DVD *First Season*. In it, Chap's client gut-shot a leopard. The video depicts several professional hunters, including Chap, tracking the wounded leopard. At the end of the video, Chap was mauled by the leopard. It is fascinating to watch but disconcerting to a client who intends to hunt leopards.

During the offseason, when not hunting, Chap is a fishing guide at a resort on the Zambezi river, specializing in leading clients on tigerfish expeditions. Tubbs and Japhet spend their offseason farming on small plots around Victoria Falls. These three Zimbabweans have worked together hunting dangerous game for ten years.

Chap, Japhet, and Tubbs

Luggage and rifle case collected, Chap Esterhuizen greeted me outside customs at Victoria Falls International. As Chap and I left the small terminal, we passed ten native dancers with a tip jar. I always stayed to watch the dancing. I wish I had videoed it. The hopping and shuffling to the sharp rhythm of the drums was reminiscent of the tribal dancing in *King Solomon's Mines*. I dropped ten dollars into their tip jar.

After flying for twenty-six hours (with an additional eight hours between flights), and only sporadic sleeping, I was damned jet lagged. It would have been pretty silly to begin hunting then, so I reserved a hut at the Gorges Lodge, a resort twenty minutes from the Victoria Falls airport. The Gorges is a collection of very luxurious one-bedroom huts with thatched roofs, sitting exactly on the edge of the cliffs overlooking the Zambezi River.

The greeting by the staff at the Gorges was delightful. My luggage was whisked away to my hut; I was offered a sweet concoction of fruit juices. After drinking it, however, I went straight to the bar, which was an open-air patio hanging directly over the cliff one hundred meters above the Zambezi. As I stood against the railing, looking down on the mighty Zambezi, the barman brought me a cold Windhoek, a lager beer brewed in Windhoek, the capital of Namibia. After my long travels, it was a fabulous treat. Finally, I'd arrived in Zimbabwe.

Chris and Chap Esterhuizen

I had the beer. Then another. Chris Esterhuizen, Chap's uncle, was the resort manager. Chris sat with me sipping an amber-colored drink in a cocktail glass. An old, grizzled Rhodesian, Chris used to manage a huge hunting concession in Northern Rhodesia (now Zambia). If a logging camp had a lion problem, Chris was called in to sort it out. In the late 1970s, Chris and Chap's father, Andre, served with Grey's Scouts, an irregular cavalry unit which fought with the minority in Zimbabwe's War of Independence.

We talked about things that were not important, but were comfortable to us, while we sipped our drinks: lion hunting, local construction at the airport, the eagles nesting in the cliffs across from Gorges, the effect that the rain up in Angola was having on the depth of the Zambezi, and a number of other similarly critical subjects.

After traveling over thirty hours and drinking two beers, I staggered off to my hut. My luggage, except for my rifle case, was in my room (rifles went to Chris's office). I fell out of my clothes, turned on the overhead fan, and opened the door to the patio overlooking the Zambezi. I then slipped between the mosquito netting and dropped into a deep, exhausted sleep.

Sometime later in the early evening I groggily woke up. I bathed, clothed, and wandered down to the open-air dining room for supper. Chap and Chris were sitting in the bar overlooking the river, waiting for me.

"Beer or wine?"

"Bottle of Windhoek."

The waiter then asked, "Zebra fillet or hippo stew?"

"Hippo stew," I said.

Served with an assortment of corn, beans, potatoes, and other vegetables, it gradually brought me back to life.

Since there were other guests in the dining room, some of whom may have been anti-hunting, Chap and I talked quietly about the upcoming hunt. There was no reason to add stress on Chris by upsetting anti-hunting guests. That was why the rifle case was in the office; we didn't want to be seen hauling rifles around.

The Gorges bar overlooking the Zambezi River

After dinner and another Windhoek at the bar overlooking the

Zambezi River, I returned to my hut. The paths from the common area to the different huts were laid with flat stone and wound through the African greenery of the areas above the cliffs of the river. It was very exotic. It made me anxious to hunt the wilds of Africa.

As I was still exhausted, I fell asleep easily.

I woke up the next morning feeling better, less jet lagged. I returned to the dining room for breakfast, ordering eggs, ham, toast, coffee, and orange juice. A young European couple was also in the dining room sharing the sunny, cool, beautiful day.

As I finished, Chap came in to get me. We were going to the town of Victoria Falls for a little excursion.

Victoria Falls is an old colonial town that was founded in 1901. The town was a way station for the never-completed "Cape Town-to-Cairo" railroad. The railroad line crossed from Southern Rhodesia (now Zimbabwe) into Northern Rhodesia (now Zambia) over the Zambezi Gorge, just south of the falls. The bridge, built for the railroad in the early 1900s, still spans the Zambezi River, but now is a center for bungee jumping. Victoria Falls has become a regional tourist town focusing on the falls, but there are good safari hunting and fishing concessions in the area.

Chap and I went into the town and walked around the old British Empire neighborhoods which, over the years, have turned into souvenir shops and beer bars. Sitting at a street-side bar, we sipped Tusker beer and watched tourists walk by. Once we finished our beers, we headed to the biggest natural attraction in all of southern Africa: Victoria Falls.

In 1855, Dr. Livingstone was the first European to see Victoria Falls. I had always wanted to visit the massive waterfall, so I paid the five-dollar entry fee, which allowed me to walk along the south edge of the gorge, opposite the falls. The mile-long walkway follows the broad reach of the falls. While it is neither the widest nor the tallest waterfall in the world, its width of one mile and the height of 110 yards make it one of the most impressive waterfalls in the world.

Chap and I walked along the edge and kept inside the low wooden barrier, becoming sodden from the never-ending spray. We passed through the area that is the only "tropical forest" in Zimbabwe, an area about an acre in size that is constantly drenched by the mist from the falls.

After twenty minutes of staring at the water rushing over the falls, as Dr. Livingstone similarly did over a century ago, we headed back.

We returned to the Gorges, sipped a beer, and prepared to go to my next "jet lag recovery" camp.

The following morning Chap and I packed up and headed off in his Range Rover to a photographic camp in the Hwange National Park. Hwange is one of the largest game parks in the world. While there are hunting blocks around Hwange National Park, there is no hunting allowed in the park itself, just as there is no hunting in America's national parks. The park is almost 6,000 square miles on the western edge of Zimbabwe. The carnivores in the park include lions, leopards, hyenas, cheetahs, Cape wild dogs, and many of the smaller cats. The park is famous for having a very large population of elephants, so many that the elephants are destroying the park. With artificial water pans built for the elephants, they come in huge numbers to drink. Unfortunately, the plant life, specifically the trees that the elephants eat, cannot keep up. When the elephants destroy the plant life, the other herbivores leave, which causes the carnivores to leave. The elephants are gradually turning Hwange National Park into a desert.

After driving three hours through the park, we arrived at the Nehimba Camp. Nehimba's setup is similar to the Gorges, with first-class sleeping huts and a fabulous common area. Nehimba's common area, however, overlooks a broad, manmade water pan, providing elephants and various plains game with ample water year-round.

Like at the Gorges, my rifle case was taken to the office, and the rest of my luggage went to my hut.

Up on the platform of the common area, with a cool greeting drink in hand, I watched a small elephant herd about a hundred yards away drink at the artificial pool. It was a typical elephant herd: the matriarch cow, several of her sisters, several calves of various ages, and a couple of breeding bulls.

Chap joined me in the common area, and we climbed into a safari sightseeing truck and headed into the park. Only licensed wildlife guides can take tourists into the park. Since Chap has a Zimbabwe Professional Hunter's License, it counted as a Zimbabwe Guide license; therefore, he was able to take me to tour the park.

We rolled through Hwange. We saw dozens of elephants but stayed away from them. These weren't zoo elephants; they were wild elephants.

We saw impalas, jackals, and birds of all sort. Then we saw giraffes. I don't like giraffes. When they see approaching hunters, giraffes seem to warn the other herbivores who are gathered around them. The other herbivores (zebras, impalas, kudu, etc.) all take off, which is annoying.

Giraffes, however, are the most beautiful, graceful animals to watch run. They have a long, looping gait that makes it look like they are running in slow motion.

We drove past an area where there were the remains of dead elephants. There were parched bones, skulls, and a few small tusks. I referred to this as Nehimba's "elephant graveyard." In Western folklore, elephants gathered to die in a hidden location, away from scavengers. This myth, however, has been proven untrue. There are no elephant graveyards. We eventually returned to the camp to avoid the heat of the day and to have lunch.

Several hours later, after a refreshing nap, Chap took me out for an evening game drive. Again, we saw many elephants, giraffes, and impalas, and we even caught a glimpse of the gray ghost—the spiral-horned greater kudu.

On the way back to the camp, in deep dusk, Chap drove slowly while I swept a torch into the darkening bush. I was looking for two shining reflective spots. When I saw the shiny eyes reflecting the light, I whispered to Chap to stop. Chap shined a stronger torch at the eyes, and we saw the darkened form of a female leopard sitting at the end of a little pond about twenty yards away. She looked at us, but she wasn't alarmed, as lights don't usually bother big cats. She dropped into a sphinx position and lapped at the water. We watched quietly. After ten or fifteen minutes, she stood, turned, and slowly walked into the now blackened bush.

When we returned to the camp, the staff told us we saw the "camp leopard." Camps often assign the "camp" designator to animals that are frequently seen around the camp. The animal is almost considered a pet.

We had dinner with several other guests. The camp rangers and staff were aware that Chap and I were hunters, but we knew not to talk about hunting. Like at the Gorges Resort, sometimes guests of photography camps don't approve of hunting, and there was no point in making their stay uncomfortable.

African martini at Nehimba

The next day I experienced another great custom at Nehimba: the late afternoon savanna cocktail party. The crew, guides, host, and servers meet with the guests out in the savanna under a spreading tree for drinks, hors d'oeuvres, and conversation. Earlier in the day, Chap and Sarah Cronje, the camp manager and wife of noted professional hunter Bruce Cronje, asked what I'd like to drink.

"Vodka martini, of course. Dirty, if possible."

Sarah didn't know what a dirty martini was, so I told her that it was a vodka martini with olive brine instead of vermouth.

"No sweat. Got you covered," she said.

Towards the end of the day, Chap and I rolled into the designated area. The other guests and the staff had gathered for this very unique cocktail party.

Sarah handed me a martini glass, a cocktail shaker, a bottle of vodka, and a packet of black olives. Black! In my vast experience with vodka martinis, I only knew of dirty martinis made with the brine of green olives, not black. So, I was taken aback.

Chap and Sarah asked about my reaction, so I told them about the green olive brine discrepancy. They were apologetic, but I said, "Nonsense, black olives are appropriate for the Dark Continent."

I mixed the vodka in the cocktail shaker with the black olive brine and ice, and I shook vigorously. To my amazement, my "African Martini" was better than the traditional green olive dirty martini. In the growing dusk, we had drinks and chatted while surrounded by some of the most dangerous wild animals in the world. To this day, I prefer African Martinis rather than traditional dirty martinis.

After several days of becoming accustomed to the time zone change, it was time to head off to the hunting camp. Chap and I went to the local airstrip to catch a charter flight on a single-engine Beechcraft.

The airstrip itself was interesting. The pilot told me that it was three miles long and two hundred yards wide. It was an emergency landing site for the US Space Shuttle. Fascinating, if true, but I've found no documentation to show that the huge strip in Zimbabwe was an emergency landing strip for NASA.

We loaded my gear and rifle case into the plane. Chap's equipment was already at the hunting camp, along with his hunting truck and his trackers, Japhet and Tubbs. Our one-hour flight to the hunting concession kept me from driving for eight hours on both the rough, poorly maintained roads of wild Zimbabwe and the hunting concession roads where there was no road maintenance, except by apprentice professional hunters.

The flight, while bumpy, was uneventful. We flew low, several thousand feet above the ground, at my request. I loved looking down at the rural terrain of Zimbabwe. I saw villages with mud huts and rough, unpaved roads. I saw walking trails between villages and children guiding several cows from watering holes to kraals, small villages surrounded by thorn bushes. The color of the terrain was red-orange, with light green or yellow spots as trees. I looked and looked, but never saw a herd of elephants or Cape buffalo. Although it was disappointing to not spot those huge animals, my experience of flying over the African savanna was exhilarating.

We circled the airstrip in the hunting concession in the Zambezi Valley, dipping down to chase an impala herd from the dirt runway. We pulled up, lined up, and landed on the now animal-free runway. Tubbs and Japhet were in the hunting truck waiting for us. After we landed, I jumped out to greet my hunting partners. Then we headed off to the camp.

The Zambezi Valley is a beautiful, wide escarpment formed over hundreds of centuries by the flow of the massive Zambezi River, which separates Zimbabwe from Zambia. The camp sat on the Ume River, a seasonally dry river which flowed into Lake Kariba, formed when the Zambezi River was dammed in the late 1950s. Near the area of the hunting camp, Lake Kariba is at least a mile wide.

The camp and hunting concession was in a semi-arid part of Zimbabwe. The Zimbabwe rainy season is during their summer months of December through March. It is absolutely rainless from April through October. This rainfall pattern made hunting in Zimbabwe's winter as close to perfect as one could hope; the temperature ranges from a low of 65ºF to a high of 90ºF, every day, with no rain and no humidity. The camp overlooked the broad expanse of the dry, sandy river and its flood-prone areas where baboons, bushbuck, and the occasional elephant wandered.

The Ume hunting camp was located towards the center of the hunting concession. The central feature of the camp, similar to the Nehimba photography camp in Hwange National Park, was a thatched-roofed, open-sided building for dining and lounging with a mahogany bar. This was known as the common room. Close to the common room was the cook room where the camp cook performed his magic, producing great meat, vegetables, breads, and desserts over an old iron stove kept hot by a never-ending supply of burning embers.

Separate from the guest buildings was a skinning shed. In addition to skinning, separating, and preparing trophy parts, the skinners also butchered meat for consumption and disposed of unwanted animal parts.

Chap sitting in the skinning shed, skinner working on nyala

There were four or five bedroom huts scattered around the well-kept grounds. Each had a double bed protected by a complete covering of mosquito netting. There were simple shelves for storing rifles, ammunition, clothes, and hunting gear. The bathroom had a basin with hot and cold running water, a flush toilet, and a shower. A boiler complex near the cook room kept our water hot by the staff constantly adding wood to the burning embers.

Another excellent feature of the hunting camp was the laundry service. Every morning soiled clothes were picked up at the bedroom suite. The clothes were washed, dried, ironed, all by hand, and returned to the bedroom. The iron itself is an old cast-iron contraption which sits on a pot of glowing ember to warm up. A hunter could literally have only two sets of hunting clothes and still go out hunting in the morning with freshly cleaned clothes.

Chap and I each had our own cabin. The hunting crew, Tubbs and Japhet, had a small self-contained camp a little way from the main area, which was and still is tradition.

After putting away my luggage, I took my rifle and a couple rounds of ammunition to the common area where Chap, Tubbs, and Japhet were waiting for me. We walked a little outside the camp to test fire my rifle. I reattached my scope to the rifle and test fired a couple of rounds to ensure all was still sighted. I realized I was as accurate as I ever was. At least, I hit the paper.

Although the hunt technically wouldn't start until the next day, we loaded into the hunting truck, Chap driving, me in shotgun, and Japhet and Tubbs on a bench mounted in the bed behind the cab. We circled the hunting concession and got a feel for the land, seeing a dazzle of zebras or a herd of impalas and startling the occasional warthog.

From their position looking over the truck, Tubbs and Japhet were able to spot game from some distance. When they spotted something, they would tap the top of the cab and tell Chap what they saw. If the trackers spotted an animal I wanted to hunt, like a zebra, we'd stop and quietly slip out of the truck, gathering our rifles and gear. Chap, Tubbs, and I would start creeping towards the zebra, and Japhet stayed with the truck. This is called "spot-and-stalk" hunting. We would spot the prey and move into a shooting position, which could take one or two hours.

The other styles of hunting I did in Africa included tracking, which is finding suitable tracks and following the animal, sometimes for hours. I also baited, which is used strictly for carnivores. This involves hanging meat, building a blind, and waiting for the animal to appear. Another method used only for lions is calling. This method broadcasts a lion roar and, thereby, attracts surrounding lions. My favorite hunting method, of course, is to get lucky and blindly walk into an animal that I want to hunt.

We drove through the hunting area, crossing wet streams and dry streams. We drove through forests of mopane, passing the occasional baobab tree.

After winding through miles and miles of Africa, we ended our day back at the hunting camp. After I returned my rifle to my hut, I strolled down to the common area. I opened a bottle of Windhoek Lager and settled into a wicker chair overlooking the dry, sandy Ume River. A hundred yards away, baboons crossed the riverbed in single file, occasionally glancing towards us. The leader of the troop led his team across the sand, occasionally letting loose with a deep-throated bark, probably warning us to leave them alone.

In the distance I saw a bushbuck: a small, spiral-horned antelope. This particular little antelope was the "camp bushbuck." Shooting him would be frowned upon, of course.

Chap joined me on the patio overlooking the Ume, and we settled into a hunting conversation, making plans for the next two weeks. We decided we would get up at five a.m., drive out at five thirty a.m., and return to camp at five p.m. for sundowners and dinner. We also decided what time in the bush we would stop for lunch.

All of this was dependent on what happened during the day, of course. If we were tracking a Cape buffalo, we wouldn't have a lunch break. If we were loading a trophy into the truck, there would be a late return. If we were waiting for a leopard in a blind, we would be very late. Develop plans, but don't expect the plans to work out.

The camp waiter rang the dinner gong, indicating it was time to eat. Dinner for us was pretty consistent throughout the hunt—meat, potatoes, green vegetables. There was always a dessert—pudding, cake, pie. The interesting part of the menu was the meat. Certainly, there was chicken or pork, but frequently we got Cape buffalo stew, zebra fried steak, or impala loins. All were excellent. The meat, even the antelope fillet, was never gamey, unlike American deer.

After dinner, Chap and I sat around the burning embers on the patio overlooking the Ume riverbed discussing life in its various forms. Dusk had fallen, and as we finished our wine, the sparkling Southern Hemisphere stars, including the Southern Cross, shined brightly down upon us. We heard the whoop of a hyena within a hundred yards and the moan of a lion two miles away.

As the fire slowly burned down, I took tremendous pleasure in knowing that I was hunting in the Dark Continent, following in the footsteps of Roosevelt, Hemingway, and Ruark.

As we retired to our respective tents, I was anxious for tomorrow's adventures.

Leopard

Big cat hunting is exasperating.

As I wrote earlier, there are five methods of hunting African wildlife: spot-and-stalk, tracking, baiting, calling, and getting lucky. There is also a seldom used variation of tracking: using dogs. It's much like American hunters using dogs for mountain lions. When the scent of the leopard is found, the hunters "release the hounds." The dogs then chase the leopard up a tree so the client can catch up and shoot the cat out of the tree. Unfortunately, there is often a high cost of dogs to be paid. Since I didn't want to use dogs, we chose to bait.

To hunt a leopard, we had to find the tracks of a male, since it is illegal to hunt female leopards in Zimbabwe. After we found tracks, we hunted a small antelope, often an impala, and hung the carcass in a tree along the leopard's route. Then, the waiting game began.

Each morning, we checked the bait we left hanging from the tree the previous day. If the bait had been hit (chewed upon) by a leopard, we built a blind within seventy yards and made sure we had a good line of sight to the hanging bait, clearing limbs and leaves out of the way. We entered the blind in mid-afternoon and waited for the leopard to come back.

There were, however, potential problems. One was we might not even find the tracks of the leopard who "owned" the territory. Another was the leopard whose tracks we found might not return to even see the bait. The leopard could also find our bait and eat some of it, but not return a second time. Even worse, he might come back to the bait but realize we're there and leave forever.

These issues made hunting a leopard problematic. Regardless of these problems, however, I loved the power, grace, and danger of leopards, so I hunted them.

After I arrived and got settled into the camp, we drove along dusty roads and searched for leopard tracks. Once we found and analyzed the tracks, determining it was male, we went to find an impala. Usually, I hunted female impalas for bait as they were more numerous than the males. I shot two female impalas, and we took them to the skinning shed to remove the guts, as leopards prefer to eat muscle. Chap and I saved the liver for a fried snack with sundowners, our evening drinks.

The next day we took the impala carcasses to two good "leopard trees" along our leopard's walking route. The "leopard trees" were big trees near leopard tracks with large branches parallel to the ground, at least fifteen feet above the ground. We suspended one of the impalas from a big limb on a tree out of the reach of lions and hyenas. Positioning the bait in this way would also force the leopard to stand on a lower limb and reach out to grab the bait with his foreleg. This prevents having to shoot a cat while he's sitting or lying, which is not ideal because it is difficult to judge where the vital organs are.

We removed branches from around the bait for sighting and bullet flight purposes. If a bullet hits a branch, it would deflect the bullet away. We also draped leafy branches over the top of the bait to keep vultures from discovering a free meal.

Leopard tree with impala bait hanging

Then our group retreated from the tree and built the blind. It was a U-shaped structure: five feet high, fifteen feet long on the three sides, and open on the side away from the bait tree. We tied tree limbs together to form the frame of the blind. We hung long grass and tree branches over the walls. We would be invisible to the leopard when it was sitting in the tree. There were two holes in the camouflaged wall, one for my rifle and the other for Chap to clearly see the situation in the tree. In addition, Chap attached an overhead light above the bait with a rheostat to control the brightness and a microphone so we could hear the leopard when he climbed the tree and ate. Chap strung the electrical wires from the tree into the blind, attaching them to a car battery he brought.

The blind was about forty yards away from the leopard tree, up a slight rise. A stream, twenty feet wide and two feet deep, separated us from the leopard tree. The setting sun was behind us, so it was a good location. Once the leopard was confident that he was alone with his free evening meal, he would settle into the tree.

At three p.m., Chap, Japhet, Tubbs, the game ranger, and I parked the truck about a mile from the blind. Leaving Tubbs, Japhet, and our game ranger in the truck, Chap and I quietly walked down to the blind. We hoped the cat was not anywhere near us. If he was, he would take off the moment he realized we were coming down.

Sitting on canvas chairs, we settled into the blind, intently looking at the impala we hoped would lure the cat into the tree. We had to be completely silent. At five forty-five, with the sun starting to set, Chap tapped me, pulling me from a light doze. He leaned over—female leopard! In Zimbabwe, female leopards are not allowed to be hunted for the protection of the species. The professional hunter would be fined $20,000 if he was responsible for shooting one. Therefore, I didn't shoot, but I did study the cat through my 4x rifle scope, ensuring the safety on my .375 was secure.

She was a beautiful adult female: slender, with a smaller head and smaller shoulders than a male. She daintily pulled meat from our bait. In the growing dusk through the trees, she became even more beautiful: absolutely orange, yellow, and black. Noticing how she glanced down, Chap whispered to me that she had her kitten on the ground, which I could not see.

After some time, as dusk continued to grow, she dropped to the ground and disappeared. After a couple of minutes, Chap stood. The female leopard and her kitten were gone. The male would not come tonight. The odor of the female and her kitten would "put him off" the tree, meaning that their odor would keep him from returning to the bait.

We climbed the slight hill behind us to the truck. While disappointed, I was pleased to have seen a female leopard.

As the truck returned to camp, Chap outlined our strategy for tomorrow.

It was likely the female would return tonight. Because she had a kitten, she would need to eat more of the impala. She probably wouldn't eat all of it, but she'd eat enough so that what remained would not entice the big male into the tree the next day. Therefore, tomorrow we needed to harvest another impala and, by midmorning, add the new bait to the tree. We'd start our waiting game again at three p.m.

The next day, while looking for a bait impala, we rattled along a rocky road across a saddle between two kopjes, small boulder hills in the flat African veld. Chap slammed on the brakes. Just ahead of us, a fifteen-foot rock python, a non-poisonous snake, was crossing the road.

Everybody jumped off the truck and, for fun, started in hot pursuit. Japhet, with his pals running behind him, grabbed the python by his tail. The python snapped around with his mouth open twelve inches wide. Japhet, along with Tubbs and our game ranger, turned and dashed away. Chap and I, watching from the truck, laughed. Since I was not hunting snakes, the rock python continued on, free of any further harassment from our hunting expedition.

Later in the morning, we returned to our leopard tree with the replacement impala. Chap and Tubbs examined the ground around the tree. Sure enough, the female leopard and her kitten had returned the previous night. We replaced the mostly eaten impala with a fresh one and spent the rest of the morning and early afternoon driving through the concession, looking for some trophy herbivore to spot-and-stalk. Mostly, though, we were just waiting for the leopard hunt to resume.

• • •

While we were searching for impala for leopard bait (and fried liver), Tubbs saw a small group in the bush. We stopped and conducted a short stalk. Under the shade of a mopane tree, Chap quietly spread the shooting sticks for me. I placed the scope's crosshairs on the heart of the little ewe impala as she slowly grazed forward.

I fired. The impala, startled by the explosion, raised her head to look at me, and bounded away, completely unharmed.

What the hell? How could I completely miss an impala standing thirty yards away from me?

Chap, Tubbs and Japhet, standing behind me, laughed. Tubbs moved forward and pointed to a small branch of the mopane tree which ended abruptly, obviously torn off. My 300 grain bullet, travelling 2300 ft/sec, heading towards the heart of an impala ewe, hit that branch, less than a quarter of an inch thick, and flew off… probably heading towards Zambia.

I began paying attention to any trees between me and my target.

• • •

Another lesson I learned about leopard hunting was that leopard bait could be vulnerable to hyenas or lions if the bait was hung too low, or to vultures if the bait could be seen from the sky. This was relatively common. On one hunt, however, I lost a leopard bait in a more unusual manner.

We had found a good leopard tree near good leopard tracks. I shot a female impala as bait, and Tubbs hung her in the tree. We built a good blind in the late afternoon. Unfortunately, when we returned in the morning, we saw that there had been no leopard the previous night, so we left to start the cycle over again.

The following morning, we returned to check on the bait impala. When we were still a half-mile from the tree, Tubbs or Japhet banged on the roof of the truck and yelled in Ndebele. Chap stopped, climbed out, and examined the tree through his binoculars and shouted, "Shit! The bait is gone!"

Chap jumped back in the truck and started for the tree. We had an experience before where a wandering group of displaced indigenous people had stolen our leopard bait for their food, so that's what I expected. When we got there, however, Japhet and Tubbs circled the tree and pointed to the tracks: lions.

"I didn't think lions could climb trees?" I asked.

"Younger lions can climb, and that's what happened. A small pride came through last night, stopped, and climbed to our bait."

Two dainty rear hooves, which still hung from the limb, were all the lions left of the leopard bait.

Since no self-respecting leopard would return to a tree with a lion scent, we no longer used that spot to hang bait.

• • •

At three p.m. we returned to the blind where we had rebaited the tree. We verified the wires for the overhead light and microphone were still in place. We were joined by Mike Blignant, an apprentice professional hunter. Like all apprentices, Mike was always willing to go with a professional hunter and his client on a leopard hunt. We gathered into the blind, settled ourselves into our chairs, and sat in perfect silence for hours as the sun went down.

At around nine p.m., with the sun down on a moonless night, Chap gently touched me. His hand was on the headphones, and he was listening intently. Chap whispered, "He's there." Chap can determine the leopard's sex by how it eats. Females pick daintily at the impala, and males chomp. The male has a much larger head and shoulders, so he has a more powerful bite. After a pause, Chap slowly turned the light's dial up, bringing on the light above the bait and exposing a big tom balancing on the limb.

At first, the leopard continued eating. Then, he suddenly stopped, leaned back, and looked around. He had become agitated, so Chap quickly turned the light off. After a few seconds with the overhead light off, Chap whispered, "He's eating again." The leopard had calmed down.

Quietly, Chap turned to Mike and handed him a big torch out of his equipment bag. "Turn this on, point it above the tree, and slowly lower the light beam. Let the cat become accustomed to it." As Mike turned on the torch and slowly lowered the light, the cat continued eating. This time the leopard ignored the light.

Switching the safety off, I centered the crosshairs of my .375 on the shoulder of the cat. The leopard suddenly stepped back on the limb, then disappeared from my scope.

"Shit," Chap muttered. Chap raised slightly, looking through his binoculars. "He's on the floor. Lower your barrel and shoot!"

I lowered the barrel straight down to the base of the tree and the leopard's ass appeared in my scope. I shifted the crosshairs to the left, and the cat was in perfect position for a shoulder shot. I pulled the trigger.

The flash of the .375 at night blinded Chap and me. Mike, however, was off to the side. He was still holding the torch on the cat and could see the situation. No longer concerned with silence, Mike shouted, "He's hit!"

I started scrambling and lurching and knocked over my chair in the process. I cleared the spent brass from my rifle and looked towards the tree.

"Wait. Wait. Wait." Chap had regained his night vision and scanned the area under the tree with his binoculars.

"Can you see him? Is he there?" I asked.

"He's not there," Chap said.

"Fuck. Let's go." I started for the open rear of the blind.

Mike said, "You hit him hard on his shoulder. He's not going far."

Chap stopped me. "This is the time to have our traditional cigarette. Let him stiffen up." We waited. We allowed the leopard to settle down so he wouldn't sprint away when he heard us approach. This would allow a severely injured cat to stay near the bait tree. I sat down, impatient to run to the tree. In the distance behind us, we saw torches bouncing down the hill. Tubbs, Japhet, and the game ranger heard the shot and were running down to join us.

"Good hit?" Chap asked Mike.

"Really good," Mike said. "I saw blood splatter behind him. The cat jumped into the long grass."

Tubbs, Japhet, and the ranger tumbled into the blind, full of questions. Chap, Mike, Japhet, and Tubbs all talked at once. Speaking in Ndebele, Chap explained the situation to the excited trackers.

Finally, after we finished our imaginary cigarette, we started to our leopard tree. Wading across the stream between the blind and the tree, we approached the tree cautiously. Tubbs examined the area and touched the sticky grass. "*Gaze ipapho*," declared Tubbs, Ndebele for the dark red lung blood: a great sign. There is another color of blood, yellow, which is bad. Yellow blood is gut blood. You do NOT want to gut shoot a leopard. While a gut-shot leopard would eventually die, he would be in excruciating pain, making him exceedingly dangerous to any villagers (or professional hunters…ask Chap!) that the leopard came across.

We pointed our torches into the long grass where the leopard had jumped immediately after being hit, apparently through the lungs. Chap handed his torch to Japhet and verified he had rounds in his .500 NE double rifle. Mike checked the chamber of his .458 Lott bolt rifle, and I shoved a new round into my .375 H&H rifle. If we didn't find the cat soon, we'd need to leave and come back tomorrow. Chasing a wounded leopard at night is too dangerous.

Chap, Mike, and I slowly approached the long grass, three across. Japhet and Tubbs pointed the torches around us so that we could see where to enter.

As we entered the long grass, Mike saw a gold and black stripe on the ground. Chap and I shifted to the left. Mike touched the leopard tail with the barrel of his rifle. No movement. The leopard had been hit in the chest, took a mighty leap, and died where he landed.

We carried the dead leopard, each holding onto a leg, from the long grass to the sand along the stream. After we took pictures, Japhet backed the hunting truck down to the beach. We loaded the leopard into the back and took off to the camp, an hour's drive away.

It was about midnight when we arrived at the camp. As my pictures show, I was exhausted. The hunting staff took care of the leopard, and I headed for my tent. After a quick shower, I literally fell into bed and was asleep within seconds.

The next morning, we brought the cat out of the camp freezer, where it was stored before skinning. Seeing the leopard under the bright sun brought about a whole new sense of wonderment. He was huge.

As I reflected on my leopard hunting, I decided I did not want to hunt any more cats, leopards or lions. The process of outthinking these damned cats is very tedious. It's a long, drawn-out affair.

Tim, Chap, and the leopard

Usually, there were no positive results. Since leopards are particular about their meat, the bait would often go bad within two to three days. When this happened, the process would start over. And then over. And then over again.

When I think back to the time when we approached the long grass where my leopard had jumped, I'm surprised that I felt no fear or anxiety. I should have been terrified, especially after having seen a video of Chap getting mauled by a gut-shot leopard. Nowadays, each time I think about going into the long grass, I feel pangs of panic. I must have been running on pure adrenaline.

There is nothing quite as exhilarating as sighting a leopard on a tree limb, making the shot, and seeing if you shot well. However, it is a very stressful experience. As I said earlier, big cat hunting is exasperating.

Cape Buffalo

An interesting fact about Cape buffalo is that when not wounded, they are as docile as cattle. When wounded, however, they are the most dangerous animal on earth. If hit poorly, they will run. The buffalo will find dark, dense vegetation, back in, and face the approaching hunters, waiting to avenge the insult of four hundred grains of lead hammered through their body.

Most professional hunters who are killed in the field are killed by poorly shot buffalo. When a nervous or inept client wounds a buffalo, the professional hunter has to "sort out" the buffalo; he must track it down and kill it, usually without the client along. When this has to be done, the professional hunter follows the blood spoor, which always leads into thick brush. As the professional hunter creeps into the brush, he has his big double rifle at the ready. The buffalo, who has incredible awareness, will wait until his stalker is within a few yards before exploding at the professional hunter.

The professional hunter will likely get a shot off. The Cape buffalo will likely swing at the professional hunter with his huge horns. If things go well, the professional hunter will bury a 500-grain bullet into the buffalo's brain. If things don't go well, the bullet will hit the thick center of the horn, known as the boss, and will not immediately kill the buffalo. The buffalo will hook his horns into the groin of the professional hunter and often rip the femoral artery apart. The buffalo will run off to die, leaving the professional hunter to bleed to death. Neither Chap nor I wanted this to happen.

There are two types of buffalo herds. One is a breeding herd: cows, calves, young bulls, and a couple of older breeding bulls. This herd can number as many as a hundred individuals. This group is less desirable to hunt as there are too many eyes and ears; it's difficult to get close enough to find a good trophy bull.

The second type of Cape buffalo herd is the "dagga boys." In this group, there will be two to four old, non-breeding bulls. Young bulls will fight the older bulls over breeding opportunities, so the old Cape buffalo will stay away from the breeding herds; they just don't want to fight for the opportunity to breed anymore. Dagga boys are the best trophies—big, worn, and old, with their genetics already passed on.

There are two methods of hunting Cape buffalo: spot-and-stalk and tracking. For me, the most enjoyable method is tracking buffalo. I love finding tracks, identifying them as a huntable animal, and then following Tubbs as he tracks the buffalo. Tracking is harder, but it seems to me a purer method of hunting than spot-and-stalk. And I like hard.

• • •

Chap, Tubbs, Japhet and I were Cape buffalo hunting in the Zambezi Valley. Tubbs found good tracks, several hours old, of a couple of dagga boys. We unloaded our rifles and water, and took off in pursuit. We wandered through the flatter portions of the Zambezi Valley, gradually getting closer. The ground was firm, the vegetation was sparse, the trees provided ample cover from the sun, so the tracking was easy. While we were not quickly catching up to the dagga boys, the tracks were promising, so we kept going.

After several hours of flat terrain, the tracks approached a 300 foot hill with 30° slopes, and, to my surprise, the tracks went up. So did we.

The side of the hill was littered with large, half buried boulders and thick trees, requiring me to scramble around, sometimes grabbing tree trunks, sometimes wedging between the boulders. How on earth did two old dagga boys make this climb? And why would they come up here?

As I became more and more exhausted, I slowed down. Chap and Tubbs slowed down, waiting for me. After a time, I knew we weren't going to catch up to the dagga boys on this track, but I wasn't going to give up. When we reached the top of the hill, Chap and Tubbs were waiting for me. Tubbs pointed to the boy's tracks, which began going downhill. The damned things got up here, and kept going.

"How long ago did they start down?"

Chap smiled, "Twenty or thirty minutes."

"Long gone," I asked?

Tubbs, smiling, said, "Long gone."

"Well, shit," I said as I sat down on the highest boulder on the damned hill. "Why would they come over this hill while they could have gone around?"

Laughing, Tubbs said, "because they were klip-buffalo."

Chap and I laughed. Tubbs was referring to klipspringer, a small antelope which lives on the vertical slopes of kjopies. We didn't chase Cape buffalo, we chased klip-buffalo.

Then we started down, following the route we took coming up. Going down was as tiring as climbing up, but maybe harder going because of the exhaustive state I was in and having to twist around trees and boulders. At least the hill slope was shaded. Small comfort.

When we got down to the flats, to my surprise, Japhet and the truck was only fifteen minutes away. We had followed the buffalo in their typical circuitous route to the "hill of death."

We didn't catch up to the dagga boys, but I learned of a new African species: klip-buffalo.

• • •

Again, we were driving around the wilderness, looking for buffalo tracks. When we rounded the curve, we came upon a typical rural village, with a dozen huts and a broad Rain Tree in front.

We pulled in to ask the locals if they've seen any buffalo around. There was a gathering of men who turned to us and began wandering over to us, seemingly in a happy, inquisitive mood. Suddenly, one of the elders came towards us, carrying a gourd of some liquid, waving his arms causing his brown drink to splash out.

He was ranting and raving, probably in Ndebele. I was taken back, but Chap started laughing and I saw the wild elder's pals were laughing and pointing and pushing each other in glee.

One of the more sober villagers came up to Chap and talked briefly with him. Nodding, smiling, Chap backed the hunting truck up, and we resumed searching the wilderness for Cape buffalo tracks.

The village gentlemen were having a beer-drinking party, and one of the elders had over-imbibed. No problem, all in good fun.

Again, we drove slowly along the dusty roads looking for dagga boy tracks. When tracks were found, the boys gathered around to determine if the right type of buffalo made the tracks. If not, we returned to the truck and continued the slow search.

Finally, Tubbs identified fairly recent dagga boy tracks. There were three old buffalo who had wandered through in the last two hours. We unloaded from the truck with our rifles. We chambered our rounds, ensured the safeties were on, and put many water bottles into our backpacks.

Chap gave final instructions to Japhet, who stayed with the truck. His instructions included where we were going, how long we expected to be gone, and which preventative maintenance to perform on the truck. There was a radio check in case we needed to tell Japhet what was happening. Finally, we took our hunting positions: Tubbs in the lead to follow the tracks, then Chap, then me, and then the camp tracker and the game ranger.

We started tracking the dagga boys. It was hard to tell whether we were catching up to them; the only way of getting an idea was testing the warmth of their dung. When we came across a pile, one of us would kick it and stick a finger into the mess to ascertain the temperature. If it was warm, the buffalo were close. Cold dung meant they were far away.

Although it was winter in Zimbabwe, the temperature was still 80°F at midmorning. The beating African sun and the tension of tracking a dangerous animal caused me to sweat profusely, making the water bottles very important.

At one point, Tubbs stopped and stared into the bush, thinking he detected a buffalo or some other animal. We froze. Tubbs relaxed and continued tracking. I released a frozen breath, resumed breathing, and continued walking.

After several hours of tracking through the Zambezi Valley with dusk approaching, Tubbs stopped suddenly. Kneeling, he motioned for us to stop and get down. He waved Chap up. Chap peered through his binoculars in the direction that Tubbs indicated and scanned through dense brush to see things I could not see. After several seconds, he sent

Tubbs back and motioned me up to him. I crawled forward, carrying my rifle in one hand.

"The dagga boys are right behind that clump of yellow bushes. Fifty yards away."

I stared through my binoculars in the direction Chap indicated. I saw nothing but didn't say so. Chap crawled forward, and I followed. We stopped behind a termite mound, a cone of hard-packed dirt ten feet tall. Chap stared into the bush with his binoculars while I stayed hidden behind the mound. He turned to me. "Two good bulls," he said. Tucking his binoculars into his shirt, Chap crawled around the mound, and I followed.

Forty yards ahead of us was an old, 1,800-pound Cape buffalo, peacefully chewing the grass. He was huge, muddy, mean, and had big, worn horns.

Chap slowly stood and spread the shooting sticks and whispered, "Take him."

I placed the crosshairs on his massive shoulder. I fired. The .375 rocked me back. With the explosion ringing in my ears, I cranked another round into the chamber. Two other buffaloes crashed through the brush, running away from the sound of my safari rifle. My buffalo staggered, then turned to run into the growing dusk. Unfortunately, I didn't have time to get a second shot off.

"Good shot. Good shot, on the shoulder," Chap muttered, watching through his binoculars.

Chap stood with his big double at the ready in case the buffalo turned back to us. Gradually, the crashing of the buffalo faded as he disappeared into the brush. Tubbs, Chap, and I went to where the dagga boy was hit. To our surprise, there was no blood on the ground at all. Since I used solid bullets, we expected the round to go completely through the buffalo. Blood flows from exit holes, not entry holes, so the bullet must not have exited.

Chap and Tubbs searched the ground, looking for some trace of blood.

"Strange. I saw the bullet hit," Chap muttered.

Chap pointed in the direction the bull had run. Tubbs led the way, carefully examining the ground, grass, and leaves. But there was still no blood, so we went forward very slowly. Finally, Tubbs looked back at us and pointed to the ground.

"He laid down here," Tubbs said. "He's sick." This meant that the bullet had done some damage after all.

Tubbs turned towards where the buffalo had fled and continued walking forward cautiously.

I began hoping that, despite the lack of blood spoor, maybe, just maybe, the dagga boy was lying ahead of us dead. I hated the thought of chasing a wounded Cape buffalo. Slowly, with my rifle at the ready, I followed Chap and Tubbs. I hoped we would walk up on him stone dead, but we didn't. Tubbs kept moving forward slowly, quietly pointing at where the buffalo had lain down.

Darkness was quickly falling when Chap called Tubbs back. It had become dangerously dark, so we were leaving. Chap tied toilet paper to a tree, marking the spot where we'd start tracking in the morning.

I climbed into the truck. I felt sick. "Did I miss the buffalo?" I asked Chap.

"No," said Chap. "You hit him. You hit him well. He's lying down because he's been hit hard. We'll return in the morning with Mike and Ian. We'll get him." Ian Wakefield was another apprentice professional hunter who would help us.

Nonetheless, the long drive back to the camp was depressing. So was the dinner. Despite Chap's words of encouragement, and Tubbs pointing out where the buffalo had lain down, shooting a dangerous animal poorly is discouraging. As I fell asleep, I still thought about the point of my aim.

The next morning was no better. I had placed the hunting team, the trackers, and the local villagers in grave danger. As Chap and I ate breakfast, Mike and Ian joined us with their heavy rifles. We were silent as we headed back to the area. We stopped about half a mile from the hanging toilet paper and got out of the truck; we locked and loaded.

We walked in silence to the hanging toilet paper. Once there, we formed our stalking formation. Tubbs was out in front following the buffalo's tracks. Chap, Mike, Ian, and I spread into a "gun line" behind Tubbs. The camp tracker and game ranger followed behind us. Although we were sneaking up on absolutely nothing, we were completely silent.

Tubbs pointed to the ground every fifteen or twenty yards, indicating where the wounded dagga boy had lain down last night. We counted five times.

The Cape buffalo was likely aware that we were coming, and he could have been on us in a flash. Being caught outside the "gun line" could be fatal. Still, I occasionally wandered wide of the "gun line." Chap whispered me back. It was hard to watch for everything (Tubbs, the face-scratching branches, a wounded eighteen-hundred-pound dagga boy) and still keep myself in position.

Suddenly, there was a crashing of brush. Tubbs flashed past us to get behind the line of rifles. The buffalo leapt up fifteen yards in front of us and dashed to the side. Four rifles exploded, followed by a fifth shot that came from Chap's second barrel. Three of us cranked a fresh round into our chambers. Chap dropped his two expended cases and slammed two fresh cigar-sized rounds into his open barrels. I started forward, but Chap stopped me. We were waiting for the buffalo to "get sick."

Chap asked, "Everybody hit him?"

"Yes."

"Yes."

I paused a moment. "Shit, I don't know."

Chap, Ian, and Mike smiled at my honesty, but I was a client, for God's sake.

After a couple of minutes, Chap sent Mike and Ian to the right. Chap and I went left, where the buffalo had actually run. Tubbs followed Chap and me. We slowly climbed a gradual hill while watching for the buffalo. As we crested the hill, Chap pointed at a dark gray shape lying on the ground in the middle of thick brush. "Put a round into him," he said.

I aimed and fired into the shoulder. I hit him. There was no reaction from the buffalo; he was dead.

Ian and Mike heard the shot and showed up within a minute. Everybody gathered around the buffalo, admiring the old, worn horns. Mike and Ian shook my hand for completing the hunt, although it felt like receiving a "participation medal." We examined the buffalo for bullet entry wounds. It looked like my shot the previous day was located correctly, but it apparently didn't exit. Solid bullets will usually exit and cause a blood trail, which was missing yesterday.

Tim and Cape buffalo

Ian went back to get the truck, and he backed it up to the buffalo. A winch was unwound from the back of the cab and tied through cuts on his rear legs. Slowly, he was pulled into the bed of the truck. When the buffalo was safely loaded, we left for the skinning shed.

Sometime later, Chap backed his truck into the skinning shed. The skinners attached chains to the rear legs of the buffalo, still laying in the back of Chap's truck. Using pulleys, they hoisted the 1800 pound buffalo up, and Chap drove forward when the huge animal was clear of his truck.

Chap parked his truck and joined me in the skinning shed. When the skinners had the buffalo completely elevated, the head skinner came over and talked to Chap in Ndebele. Chap turned to me and asked, "shoulder mount only?"

"Yeah, just the shoulder mount."

He turned to the head skinner and nodded. Chap then pointed out my initial bullet entry wound and asked the skinners to look for the bullet.

Japhet wandered into the skinning shed carrying his knife.

The head skinner and his fellows began sharpening their long, thin knives, slapping them on bars or grinding a stone against the knife's edges. One of the skinners handed Japhet a sharpening bar, who began slapping his knife to draw out a razor's edge from his ancient knife.

Turning to the massive beast hanging in the air, the skinners began slicing him open. After a very short time, the dangling monster unleashed a torrent of guts spilling onto the concrete floor.

Japhet reached into the steaming mess and pulled out the string of small intestines. He cut off a four- or five-foot section, giving him a long tube of intestine.

He took the hose of running water and cleaned the outside of the intestine. After cutting the length of intestine into two sections, he turned each tube inside out, and washed it clean of undigested plant matter. He tied off each length of intestine on one end. Using his extremely sharp knife, Japhet began cutting very small pieces off the hanging Cape buffalo which he stuffed into a tube of intestine. When each was full of pieces of buffalo, Japhet drained a bloody liquid into each tube. He tied off the other end of each length of intestine.

As he left, he turned to me, holding up his tubes of buffalo meat, and said "sausage."

Chap smiled and said "Tubbs and Japhet will lay them on coals tonight and have a buffalo sausage better than anything you'll have in America."

"We'll get some of this buffalo to eat?"

"Sure," Chap replied. "We'll get some great steaks, but the rest go to local villages. That's one reason that the villagers love us hunting in their areas. It's the only protein they get."

Chap and I joined Ian and Mike in the open dining area overlooking the Ume River. Over coffee, we relived the hunt. After thirty minutes, a skinner came over. He called Chap, talked to him for a minute, and handed Chap two small objects.

Chap walked over to me. "Here's your bullet," he said. "It broke in half as it entered. Half lodged into the left lung, and half went into the stomach."

"I'll be damned," I said. "It wasn't a bad shot?"

"Nope. Excellent shot. Bad bullet."

• • •

There is a funny side story to this buffalo hunt. The morning we went to track down the wounded buffalo, Ian brought his little mix-breed terrier, Sibilobilo, with him. Sibilobilo joined us, trailing the shooting line, as we pursued the Cape buffalo.

Ian and Sibilobilo

When the shooting started, all attention turned to the buffalo. At the end of the buffalo hunt, resulting in a dead dagga boy, Ian looked for his little dog, which was nowhere to be found.

When Ian returned to the truck to bring it to retrieve the buffalo, who was standing next to the truck? Little Sibilobilo! He ran from the sound of fire and found his way back to the truck for safety.

Ian was greatly relieved.

Elephant

The African animal I've wanted to hunt the most is the bull elephant, the continent's most iconic beast.

There are two types of elephant hunting tags available to the African hunter. The first is a tuskless elephant tag, for either bull elephant or cow. As indicated by the name of the tag, this is not a hunt for trophy ivory. Elephants not growing tusks are caused by a genetic flaw, so country elephant managers don't want them to pass on their genes. The cost of this tag is considerably less than a tag for a tusked elephant. The only reward for a tuskless tag is the hunt itself.

The second elephant tag is a trophy tag. This is for a bull elephant with tusks and is the elephant hunt I wanted. We focused on old, non-breeding bulls with significant ivory. With his genetics passed on, hunting an old, non-breeding elephant would not adversely affect the species as a whole; the bull has completed his breeding mission.

I was hunting for my elephant in the Ngamo teak forest, in western Zimbabwe, which borders the Hwange National Park. Teak trees, a tropical hardwood, are tall and straight. Teak forests are spacious and, with their canopy of leaves, are cool to walk beneath.

We left the camp at five thirty a.m. to look for our bull elephant. We drove slowly along the five-mile-long dirt roads that crisscrossed the forest while Chap, Tubbs, and Japhet watched for elephant tracks. We stopped when Tubbs saw tracks and tapped the roof. We then climbed out to study them.

It was pretty easy to identify the tracks we wanted. Bull elephant front tracks are oblong while female front tracks are round. As an elephant ages, its tracks become smoother because the etched soles on the bottom of its feet wear down. So, we were looking for smooth bull front tracks more than two feet in length.

When we saw an old bull elephant track heading into the African bush, we gathered our rifles and supplies and followed it. Tubbs led the group tracking the elephant. Chap was next with me, the game ranger (and his poacher-killing AK-47) and Phinias (the camp tracker) following behind.

The game ranger is a requirement for all hunts. It's his role to ensure that Zimbabwean Fish and Game rules are followed. He would occasionally help on some aspects of a hunt (carry water or scout), but mostly he just tagged along and wrote reports at the end of the day.

The camp tracker worked permanently for a hunting camp. He was an expert in the terrain of the hunting concession and knew the general locations of different animal species. He helped with all aspects of a hunt, assisting the professional hunter's staff with trail information, and telling us which smaller species (honey badger, porcupine) could be hunted and which could not in this concession.

We followed Tubbs as he tracked our elephant using methods passed down from the day of the San people, the first hunter-gatherers of southern Africa. Occasionally, he stopped to consult with Chap or Phinias. Our pace was slow, between two and three miles per hour. The elephant we followed sometimes went over rocky ground, leaving no tracks. We'd stop, rest in the shade, and drink water while Tubbs went ahead to relocate the tracks.

Because it was winter in Zimbabwe, it was 80ºF. Between the constant walking and my anxious fear of what we'd find at the end of the tracks, it was hard, nervous work for me. The teak forest was flat with firm, sandy soil, so at least it was easy walking.

We walked for hours. Every time we came upon a pile of elephant dung, we'd test its temperature. As we got closer to the elephant, the dung got warmer. We knew the dung was from our old elephant because the dung's composition was "twiggier" than a younger elephant's dung. As elephants age, their digestive systems become less efficient and can no longer break down the mopane leaves, twigs, and bark before they pass them.

Phinias, camp tracker at Ngamo hunting camp

Finally, Tubbs confirmed with Chap and Phinias that we weren't catching up to the elephant we were tracking. After four hours of tracking, we called off this hunt. Phinias, who was extremely familiar with the concession, used the radio to contact Japhet, who was waiting back at the truck. Phinias passed directions to Japhet and led us off at an angle to meet Japhet at the nearest road.

This track was disappointing, but hunting elephant is a very unpredictable activity.

It was lunchtime. Chap and I sat in the shade and had sandwiches, boiled eggs, cold sausage links, and warm Coke. Japhet, Tubbs, Phinias, and our game ranger settled around a small fire where they cooked their sadza, a traditional gruel made of maize.

After eating, we spread a canvas to rest, occasionally dozing. High above, a dozen vultures slowly circled, searching for dead animals.

An hour passed. We got up, packed, and resumed slowly driving the crisscrossing dirt roads of the forest until we found old male elephant tracks. Again, we unloaded gear. Again, we walked in single file, following the bull elephant.

This time we caught up. An old bull elephant slowly flapped his huge ears standing in the shade of an enormous tree. Chap and I crept to about one hundred yards from him. We were silent and made sure the wind kept blowing from him to us, as elephants have superior senses of hearing and smelling.

Chap quietly cursed. This old guy had one tusk; the other had been broken off at the lip. We slowly backed away. His one tusk was of good size, maybe sixty pounds, but since I wanted two tusks for my first trophy elephant, there was no point in disturbing him. Once we were a safe distance away, we called Japhet for a pickup.

It was too late in the day for another elephant track, so we headed back for beer on the patio with strips of impala liver fried with garlic. I preferred my liver strips to be crispy, while Chap liked his soft. After dinner, we heard the African carnivores roaring, coughing, whooping, and moaning, warning others of their location in the growing night.

The next morning, we were back on the road looking for an old bull elephant. Just like yesterday, we found big bull elephant tracks. We tracked until we realized we weren't catching up—three times.

We headed out again the next morning, hoping we would finally catch up to a trophy I could proudly take home to display beside my fireplace to reminisce of my days in Africa. Like the previous days, we found and followed tracks, but this time we caught up. To our surprise, we found our old one-tusked friend standing under a different tree. Chap, Tubbs, and Phinias gathered around his tracks to memorize his sole pattern so we wouldn't track an elephant we were not going to shoot. Again, Phinias led us to the closest dirt road while Japhet was guided to our pickup location.

After going back to the dusty roads crisscrossing the Ngamo teak forest, we stopped for lunch. As we settled down, we were beset by a horrible insect species: mopane bees. They are tiny, gnat-like stingless bee which gathered by the millions (?) around my face. They invaded my ears, nose, corners of my eyes, and the corners of my mouth. They made a terrible tiny buzzing sound deep in my ear channels. They were absolutely intolerable. Waving my hands in front of my face did nothing. If I walked at a reasonable pace, the bees would fall behind, but when I stopped, they regathered to drive me insane. Chap came over with a head net in his hand. The net was similar to mosquito nets used around the lakes in the northern states. I trotted forward to leave my tormenters behind as I slid the net over my head.

Thank God!!

After eating an uncomfortable lunch, we resumed searching for elephant tracks. Over several hours, we found tracks, but not what we wanted. Eventually we returned to camp, where we rested on the patio with Windhoek beer and fried impala liver. In the growing dusk, we listened to the dangerous carnivores as they spoke to us.

The next day we again drove the dusty roads of the Ngamo teak forest, looking for promising elephant tracks. We found the tracks we wanted pretty early in the morning. We followed these particular tracks for several hours, crossing all sorts of terrain. We went up hills, down hills, and across the face of hills. We went through forests and across savannas. Although there were spring-fed streams in the area we were chasing this elephant, we mostly crossed sandy, dry rivers. The worst situation was when the damned elephant went down the sandy riverbeds. Walking through the sandy riverbeds meant having the sand pull mercilessly at my boots. Several times our elephant crossed the tracks of a herd of cow elephants. In typical elephant herds, the matriarch cow elephant leads, and the other female elephants, various aged calves, and some young bulls follow. Tubbs eventually found our bull's tracks past the cow herd's tracks, and we were off again.

Our hunting procession stopped as Tubbs looked around and pointed to various tracks on the ground. "Askari!" he whispered to Chap. The bull we were following had an escort of three askari. When young bulls begin reaching sexual maturity, the cows kick them out of the herd. The young bulls wander around, sometimes attaching themselves to the old, non-breeding bulls. These young bulls are called "askari," a term originally meaning indigenous soldiers serving in a colonial army.

The askari learn how to be dominant from the old bull, growing into aggressive, confident, mature bulls, while the askari provide additional security and companionship for the old bull.

We'd been on their trail for six hours under the equatorial sun when Tubbs came to a complete stop and peered through the mopane and teak trees. He looked back at Chap and gestured, "There he is."

Tubbs' job was done. Tubbs and Phinias quietly slid to the rear, standing behind cover. Chap checked the load on his big double and looked at me. I slowly, quietly verified there was a round in the chamber of my rifle.

Chap peered through his binoculars into the mopane undergrowth among the tall, slender teak trees. He quietly lifted a small plastic squeeze bottle from a pocket in his shorts. A squeeze produced a puff of white powder, which drifted in the slight breeze, showing the direction of the wind. It was important that we weren't in a position that would allow our scent to waft towards the elephants. If they smelled us, they would explode away.

Gradually, I heard the chewing of branches by several elephants. They were pulling branches off trees and shoving them into their mouths. The old elephant and his askari were completely unaware we were there.

Chap whispered, "His tusks look okay. Maybe forty-five pounds. We'll need to circle him to make sure he's got two complete tusks."

We also had to locate his askari. We did not want to focus so much on the old bull that we walked into a young bull in the process.

We found all four elephants were within a fifty-yard circle of each other. We could now focus on the old bull, and he was *really* old. His skin was sagging, his eyes looked tired, and, as we noticed while tracking him, his digestive system was not working well, as his dung had undigested vegetation.

He had both of his tusks. His left tusk was long and sharp, but his right tusk was shorter and worn at the end. This meant that he was "right-handed." Over the years he had used his right tusk to dig in the dried, sandy rivers to reach down for water.

Although his tusks were neither especially heavy nor long, I decided I wanted to take him. His tusks were interesting and had character, and, more importantly, he was not a breeding bull.

By now, Chap and I were standing quietly in the shade, with the wind blowing from the elephant toward us with the old bull slowly walking straight at us, pulling leaves off the mopane trees. His askari were spread out; none were closer than thirty yards away.

Chap slowly set up the shooting sticks, making sure the old bull didn't see the movement, and I rested my .375 on the sticks for stability. I slowly released the safety. The old bull was not looking towards us, even as he walked straight at us. Our position was ideal for a frontal brain shot. When he got within thirty yards, I let go, perfectly between and just below the line of his eyes.

If an elephant is shot in the brain, his rear legs will collapse first, followed by his front legs. Within a second of my shot, my bull's rear legs started to collapse, but, to my shock, he recovered! He climbed back up with his front legs. I couldn't let him get away. Since I had drawn blood, this was my elephant, whether he died or not.

As my elephant staggered back up, he was now sideways to me. Knocking over the shooting sticks, losing my hat, and cranking another round into the chamber, I ran toward the elephant. At ten yards I fired into his front shoulder, aiming into the heart and lung cavity. He staggered as I cranked my third and last round into my rifle's chamber. The elephant was quartering away, so I aimed at where his heart was positioned in his body and fired again.

I turned to Chap, who was following me with his heavy double (my life insurance) and yelled to him that my rifle magazine was empty. Reaching down to the cartridge holder on my belt, I pulled three more .375 solids and shoved them into the magazine. I didn't drop one. Slamming the bolt forward, I turned back to the bull. He had reeled around, so I was now facing his rear. I ran around him and got closer. From five yards away, I fired again into his heart and lung cavity.

He finally dropped and rolled onto his side. His chest was no longer expanding. Chap stepped beside me and told me to touch his open eye with my barrel. If he flinched, he was still living. If not, he was dead.

No flinch.

I was exhausted. I had followed Tubbs for hours during the tracking process, studied the situation for an hour once we were in place, and then endured fifteen seconds of terror before finally taking the elephant down. I took the final round out of my chamber and slowly, exhaustedly walked back to pick up my expended brass.

Tim's elephant

Phinias ran over to me. "You're an action man," he said. I looked quizzically at him. "Most hunters shoot and back up. You shoot and charge."

I was tempted to tell him that since I didn't shoot well enough, I had to clean up my mess or lose the elephant altogether. But I didn't. I just grinned.

Then Tubbs and the game ranger (still carrying his AK-47) ran over, and there were hugs and handshakes all around. We called Japhet to bring the truck through the forest.

As Chap was studying the tusks, measuring the diameter with his hands, it occurred to me to ask, "What happened to the askari?" Until that minute I had completely forgotten about them.

"On the first shot, they all scattered," he said.

"Christ!" I said. "That could have been a disaster."

"Yeah, but I was watching for them," Chap said, turning to me.

"Young bulls take off. A cow wouldn't have. She would have run towards you. Could have been a dangerous situation, but it wasn't."

Oh, I thought. This wasn't dangerous…?

Japhet drove up quicker than I expected. It turned out that we had been following the bull and his askari in broad circles, which, of course, everybody knew but me.

Now it was time to return to camp to get the butchers, men who would carve up two tons of meat. I was concerned, of course, about leaving the ivory for a poacher to steal.

"Won't happen," said Chap. Apparently, poachers tend to stay away from hunting concessions.

On our thirty-minute drive back to camp, I fell asleep awkwardly against the window. As we drove into camp, Chap honked his horn, pulling me awake. The camp manager and his assistants ran out to get the news. Phinias told the "head butcher" exactly where the old bull was laying. We got more water bottles and headed back to my elephant. The camp tracker directed us on a different path to the elephant, a quicker path. As we went through the forest, Tubbs, Japhet, Phinias, the game ranger, and I used machetes to hack a vehicle path to the elephant. After an hour of exhaustively cutting a trail for the butchers to follow, we arrived back at the bull. To my relief, the tusks were still there. We sat in the shade and dozed while we waited for the butchers. In thirty minutes, an old but workable tractor pulled up with a long flatbed trailer in tow. The trailer carried twenty men, all with machetes and knives.

The driver moved the trailer to within ten yards of the elephant and then unhitched it from the tractor. Five men climbed on the elephant and started cutting and removing the skin in big sheets. When the elephant was half skinned, they hooked the tractor to him to turn him over and finish skinning. As the skin was removed, huge slabs of meat were cut off and loaded onto the trailer. This meat was a windfall for the local villagers, providing them with weeks of free protein that was ordinarily unavailable to them.

Elephant butcher preparing meat for the crew

Several small cooking fires, including one by Japhet, were started a short distance from the elephant, each burning down to a bed of hot embers. Japhet sliced off a two- or three-pound piece of meat from the elephant's temple and took it to his fire. He cut the meat into cubes and made "elephant kabobs" with potatoes, tomatoes, and onions. In a short while, our hunting team and I were eating delicious elephant meat. At the other fires, the butchers had their meal, which was also elephant meat cooked on hot embers.

As time passed, Chap talked to the head butcher and told him what parts of the elephant were to be preserved for me—tusks and so many square yards of skin. Shortly after that, we headed back to camp.

When we arrived back at the hunting camp, I joined Chap in the common room for my Windhoek and exciting, unending talk about the hunt. We had dinner, and I collapsed onto my bed. My elephant adventure was over.

The next morning, I examined the tusks and the skin, which was now salted. Cuan Meredith, the taxidermist in Bulawayo that I used, would be along to gather my elephant parts for treatment before sending them to me in America.

Other Hunts

Impala

The impala, which is generally the size of America's white-tailed deer, is, I believe, the most frequently hunted animal in Africa. Not only do I have three shoulder mount trophies (two rams and one ewe), I have also harvested at least a dozen impalas to be used as leopard bait and camp meat. When hunting bait impalas, ewes are the most commonly shot because they cost less, and there are so many of the damned things.

Tim and impala

Impalas are pretty easy to locate in Zimbabwe. They are literally everywhere. The most interesting group Chap and I saw was a bachelor herd of fifty or sixty, all with nice, mature horns.

Impalas are my second favorite animal to watch run, behind giraffes. When they run, they make long, high leaps into the air. The herd, when attacked by predators, scatters in different directions. The high leaps increase the chance of survival for the ones who are the strongest and most agile.

They are also great to eat. Impala liver was one of my favorite African treats. I loved overlooking the Zambezi River eating my fried impala liver with a vodka martini. Add to that the whooping of the hyenas and the moaning of the lions, it was nothing short of perfect.

Hyena

My favorite African animal is the hyena. It is feared, hated, admired, misunderstood, and somehow both physically ugly and physically beautiful.

When animals are discussed in early African literature, hyenas are consistently the most incorrectly described. Early (1880-1940) written descriptions of the hyena depict a cowardly, misshapen, sniveling thief, completely unable to hunt for itself. Hemingway, in particular, seemed to despise them. On his first safari, he mercilessly killed every hyena he came across, which was reportedly over thirty.

However, absolutely none of these descriptions are correct. While it will scavenge or eat leftover meat if the opportunity arises, as will any carnivore, hyena is a superior hunter and kills as much as eighty percent of its food.

The hyena has a loping gallop caused by enormous front shoulder and neck muscles. These shoulder and neck muscles give it one of the strongest bites in the animal kingdom. Hyenas can even eat bones, which causes their scat to be white.

While many identify hyena vocalization as a laugh ("laughing hyena"), hyenas only laugh, or cackle, while socially eating. Their most common communication is a "whoop," which carries long distances at night. It is terribly exciting to hear hyenas "whooping" at each other while having sundowners over a campfire at night. The hyena's whoop is every bit as intimidating as the lion's moan, as there are more hyenas whooping than lions moaning, and the hyenas can be close. Very close.

There are four hyena species in southern Africa: the spotted hyena, the brown hyena, the striped hyena, and the aardwolf. In Zimbabwe, the only hyena allowed to be hunted is the spotted hyena. There are two ways to hunt the spotted hyena: being lucky (suddenly walking up on one) and baiting. Baiting hyenas is slightly different from baiting the big cats as the bait is placed on the ground and chained in place. If this is not done, the hyena will tear apart the carcass and carry the meat in different directions. The meat does not need to be fresh (or anything close to fresh), as hyenas will eat meat in any condition. Cats, as an aside, are very particular about the condition of their meat, which needs to be only slightly fresh.

One afternoon, Chap and Tubbs found hyena tracks on a dry, sandy riverbed. While I had not specifically been hunting hyenas, I was excited to have the opportunity to hunt them. Chap pointed to a bluff across the sandy river overlooking the hyena tracks, noting that was where we would put up the blind. He also found a suitable tree with low branches that kept vultures away and a thick trunk on the bank of the riverbed to anchor the bait. We had just finished a leopard hunt and had extra junk meat. We had old half-pieces of impala, a haunch of a zebra, and remains of a baboon. While Tubbs and Japhet wired and chained the rotting meat to the tree, Chap and I built the blind on the bluff, close to the edge of the cliff. The blind wasn't as sturdy as the ones used for leopards because it was basically just brush tied to a log and hung between two trees a few yards from the fall-off to the sandy river twenty yards below. It was not a blind we would spend hours in; it would just be a place to sneak into early in the morning so we could look down on the bait and, hopefully, see hyena.

The next morning, we stopped the truck about a half-mile from our blind and quietly walked forward in the early morning light. As we approached the blind, Chap stopped me and listened for the whoop or cackle of a hyena, but there was nothing.

"They might have left," Chap whispered.

We crawled up to the blind and peered through the brush. The meat was mostly gone, and the chain was still in place, but there were no hyenas.

"Well, shit."

We sat down staring at no hyenas, when suddenly, from up the sandy riverbed, we saw a jackal peering cautiously, gradually inching closer to the remaining meat. This black-backed jackal looked like a cross between a German shepherd and a fox.

"Do you want a jackal?" Chap asked.

"Sure," I said, as I prepared to shoot.

The jackal was whimpering, dashing back and forth about twenty yards from the remains of the hyena meat.

"Hold on," Chap whispered. "The jackal's barking is pulling in a hyena."

Suddenly, the jackal turned and dashed away in the direction from which he came. A big hyena ambled out of the brush and made a short run at the vanishing jackal.

"Take the hyena!"

From fifty yards, I fired. The hyena collapsed on the sand. I cranked another round into my .375.

"Hold. Don't shoot."

The tail of the hyena rose and then flopped on the sand. We waited and watched the flattened hyena, anticipating movement. Hearing the rifle shot, Tubbs and Japhet drove down behind us, came to the blind, and looked down at the still hyena. Without speaking, we turned, climbed into the truck, and drove down the twisty road to the riverbed.

Tim and hyena

This hyena was a big, old male. His muzzle, head, and shoulders were scarred. Hyena society is a matriarchal society; female hyenas are generally bigger than the males. Even compared to the females, however, this was a large hyena. This old boy had been through the wars.

Back at camp, the skinners went to work on him. I ended my hyena hunt with a very handsome trophy of my favorite African animal.

Rogue Elephant

There is a non-tag elephant that can be hunted, but the hunt cannot be planned in advance. It's the "problem animal control" (PAC) elephant, also referred to as a rogue elephant. Typically, when an elephant threatens a village, the village elder notifies the local governing body, the Council. The Council then contacts the closest professional hunter, who is expected to break off his hunt to dispose of the elephant in question. The professional hunter, or his client, kills the elephant, but no part of the rogue elephant can be taken by the professional hunter or client. All parts, including tusks, are owned by the Council, and nearby villages get all the meat.

One bright morning while resting in camp, Chap came to me with a unique situation. The local Council had informed him that an elephant had created a PAC situation by threatening a village. Because Chap was recovering from a strained back, he asked Mike Blignaut if he'd take me, along with Tubbs and Japhet, to "sort out" the elephant problem. I was excited! There was nothing more challenging than hunting elephants. We jumped into Chap's truck with Mike behind the wheel.

Unfortunately, PAC regulations required us to take government rangers with us. We drove to a local ranger compound to pick them up. When we got there, the rangers seemed aware of the situation but were in their morning disarray, standing around half-dressed while chatting around a fire. I couldn't tell if they didn't want to go, but they were certainly showing little interest.

Finally, Mike rousted four of them into their clothes. They got their AK-47s from the guard shack and reluctantly climbed into the back of the truck.

As we drove to the endangered village, we came upon a mongrel dog trotting along the road. Mike slammed on the brakes, jumped out, grabbed his .22 Mag rifle, and shot the dog in the ass. The dog took off into the brush. The lead ranger grabbed his AK-47, jumped off the truck, and disappeared into the brush following the dog. Very shortly after, we heard the rifle fire. Minutes later, the ranger came back to the truck, said, "OK, dog dead," and jumped aboard. Mike started up again.

"What was that all about?" I asked.

"Dogs away from villages are owned by poachers. We always kill them on sight."

Shortly after, we drove into the small village that reported the elephant. Mike, Tubbs, Japhet and the head ranger talked to the village headman, who described the elephant and the specific area where he had last been seen.

After driving to the last reported location of the elephant, we parked the truck and stumbled into our hunting order. Tubbs took the lead followed by Mike, me, and the ragtag group of rangers.

Tubbs quickly found the tracks and pointed out something strange.

The elephant's right rear track was dragging; he wasn't able to lift his right rear leg. This was what made him dangerous; he was injured and probably in pain.

As we followed the tracks of the elephant, Tubbs, Mike, and I fell into our disciplined hunting string, but the rangers started wandering around. They sat. They walked off to examine a strange tree. They stopped to look into streams. One ranger actually made a cell phone call, which infuriated Mike. He offered to smash the phone, so the call was quickly terminated.

After a few hours of tracking the elephant, Tubbs motioned Mike and me forward. The elephant, a young male, was standing on three legs in the shade of a grove of trees. He was holding his right rear leg off the ground.

In the shade of the trees, Tubbs spread the shooting sticks. I placed my .375 on the sticks and fired into the front shoulder of the elephant. He lurched to the side. Mike ran up beside me and also shot into the elephant's shoulder. Mike's rifle shot literally knocked me on my ass. Mike's .458 Lott had a muzzle break on the end of his barrel, a series of slits in the barrel that reduces recoil for the shooter. Unfortunately, the energy saved from recoil is transformed into noise and sideways muzzle pressure.

As I staggered to my feet, Mike helped me up, asking if I was okay.

"I'm fine. I'm fine," I said as I recovered and readied my rifle to shoot the rogue elephant again.

I realized I had no hearing in my right ear, just a slight buzz, but I fired again at the staggering elephant. Mike stepped in front of me and fired. Since this was a PAC elephant, there were no sporting considerations for me, the client. We were here only to take care of a problem. The young elephant started to drop. Mike and I both repositioned ourselves and fired another volley into his shoulder. The injured elephant died.

Mike came back to me. "Are you alright? God, I'm sorry."

"No, no, I'm fine," I said, although I couldn't hear with my right ear.

Mike, Tubbs, and I went to the elephant. He was a young male, probably around twenty. His tusks were about twenty inches long and very skinny. We looked at his right rear leg. Halfway between the bottom of his foot and his knee, his leg was bent the wrong way. It was obviously broken, and there was pus seeping from the wound. He must have been in terrible pain.

Mike and Tubbs concurred that the young elephant must have stepped into a wire snare in the past three months. Because of the poor economy and institutionalized sustenance farming, many rural Zimbabweans add to their food supply by putting snares out to catch antelope. In sustenance farming, the owner of the five-acre plot will eat what they grow and grow only what they eat. Some farmers will be lucky enough to have a cow or two, but they seldom have any other form of food. These snares the villagers put out for antelope are critical to their survival. Our PAC elephant must have stepped into a snare anchored to a tree and pulled until he broke the snare, as well as his leg.

Japhet drove to the local village with the news that the elephant was here for them to butcher. Within fifteen minutes, Japhet drove up with the elders in the back of the truck. Ten minutes after that, a string of villagers streamed in, carrying knives, axes, baskets, and canvas sacks. Japhet quickly organized the mob. Eight adult men with knives and axes attacked the elephant, cutting off skin and hunks of meat that were thrown into growing piles. Other men, women, and children sat in the shade of the trees, gossiping and enjoying themselves, looking forward to heaping piles of cooked protein.

Tim, Mike, and rogue elephant. Note: the right rear leg is broken

This went on for an hour. Mike, Tubbs, Japhet, and I sat in the shade and watched. Everything but the tusks and the trunk went to the villagers. Even the intestines, which were turned inside out and washed, were thrown onto the meat pile. When the carnival was over, we took the tusks and trunk to the Council Chief's enclosure. The trunk, as it turns out, is a desired piece of meat that always goes to the chief.

That was the end of my rogue elephant experience. No wild charging elephant tearing into the line of baggage-carrying coolies, and no whipping of tusks at the brave "great white hunters." Instead, just a young elephant with a broken leg that needed to be put down.

Greater Kudu

One of the most iconic animals in Africa is the greater kudu (and yes, there is a species named lesser kudu). The greater kudu entered public awareness as the subject of Hemingway's classic *The Green Hills of Africa*. Greater kudu are elk-sized antelope with tall, spiraling horns. A large kudu will have horns sixty inches long. Greater kudu are a destination prey, meaning that hunters will come to Africa specifically to hunt them. In my case, it was a spot-and-stalk creature. If we saw a good, mature male, I wanted to make every effort to hunt him. If not, that was fine, because I didn't come to Africa for a greater kudu.

Tim and greater kudu

Once, during an elephant hunt, while driving from one section of the concession to another, Tubbs tapped on the top of the car and said, "*Mbelabala*," kudu in Ndebele. Chap stopped, jumped out, and looked through his binoculars to where Tubbs had pointed.

"Good kudu, yeah?"

We started moving towards a kjopie (Boer for a tall, rocky mound in the middle of a flat savanna and pronounced "kopy"). Chap led, but he wasn't really tracking; we were just trying to keep up with the kudu. Through the brush we saw that the kudu was outrunning us. Chap stopped to spread the shooting sticks.

"Get ready. He'll climb the kjopie."

Resting my rifle on the sticks, I looked above my scope at the rocky hill ahead of us. As the kudu climbed the kjopie, he stopped and turned to look back at us.

Chap calculated and said, "About a hundred yards away, twenty yards up."

I put the crosshairs just above his shoulder and fired.

"He's down," Chap yelled. "Let's go."

We ran towards the kjopie. Tubbs, of course, outdistanced us. As Chap and I began climbing the kjopie, Tubbs reappeared, whooping with pleasure. I climbed up to the dead kudu. He was old. He had scars and worn shoulders, and his horns were cracked and stained.

In order to get the kudu to the truck, we had to wrap a tarp around him and drag him down the kjopie.

That evening we had great kudu chops.

Nyala, Bushbuck

Nyala and bushbuck are two of Africa's nine spiral-horned antelope species, which also includes the greater kudu. Both the bushbuck and the nyala are found in Zimbabwe, and both are spot-and-stalk antelope. The bushbuck is three feet tall, and the nyala is four feet tall. While it is my opinion that neither are destination species, they are still both beautiful and delicious and worth the hunt if the opportunity presents itself. Their gracefully spiraling horns make for stunning shoulder mounts.

Chap took me to southern Zimbabwe, specifically to hunt nyala. We settled into a hunting camp in the lowveld adjacent to the Bubye River. The Bubye is a tributary to the Limpopo River, which separates Zimbabwe from South Africa. When we got there, we went into our normal camp arrival routine: moved our bags into our huts, went to the range to test fire my rifle, and prepared for the hunt.

The next day Chap and I followed Tubbs as we stalked a nyala. It was early April, and the summer rains had just ended in Zimbabwe, so everything was green. The bushes were large, green, and round, and the grass was lush, green, and long.

As we crept around a large bush, I stepped into a deep hole that was covered with the dense grass. As I fell, I twisted my body to protect my scope. I saved my scope, but I landed squarely on my right shoulder. I woofed in pain and lost the nyala. The fall resulted in a damaged rotator cuff and detached bicep that required surgery when I returned to America.

Tim and nyala

After several days of fruitless searching, Tubbs, Chap, and I followed three nyala into the thick brush. Chap and I moved out away from the brush to prepare for the nyala to exit. Tubbs kept moving forward into the brush to drive the nyala out.

We were about fifty yards from the end of the dense brush when Chap threw up the sticks; I positioned my rifle, ready to shoot. Chap moved a little to my right, which allowed him to get a good view of the nyala as they left the brush.

"Not the first one," he said, looking at each as they left the brush and entered the open space. "Not the second one. The third—hit him."

I saw a very well-horned bull nyala trotting away from us. He was three-quarters facing away from me when he stopped and looked back. I put the crosshairs at a point behind his rib cage on the line to his heart and fired. He dropped.

Chap grabbed the sticks, and we ran to the nyala, which was laying stone dead.

Chap turned him over. The angle of the shot was so extreme that the bullet burned a path along the skin before it entered. It was the best shot that I've ever made and ended up being a great trophy.

An interesting situation occurred at the nyala camp. We were joined at the camp by two professional hunters and a client. The client was an American, from Texas, hunting leopard with bow in an area near where I was hunting nyala. He normally hunted in South Africa, but Zimbabwe had more leopards, and more leopard tags, so he brought his South African professional hunter with him to hunt leopard. As he was hunting in Zimbabwe, he was required to have a Zim PH. On a few mornings, before we all took off, I watched him practice bow shooting. Apparently, his range was about 40 yards. He seemed accurate, so I wasn't surprised when Chap and I were told that he shot his cat.

I was sorry he left to return to South Africa before I could talk to him. I would have loved to hear his story.

Next to be hunted was the bushbuck, a beautiful little spiral-horned antelope similar to the nyala, except smaller. Bushbuck are very common to both the savanna and the forests, and they are definitely spot-and-stalk antelope. I had always wanted one, but the opportunity had never presented itself.

We were driving out of camp one morning when Tubbs spied a bushbuck. We continued on our intended hunt, but Chap noted his location. Bushbuck live within a very limited range and seldom leave their small territory.

On our way back to camp in the evening, we slowed so Tubbs and Japhet could watch for the bushbuck. When we pulled into camp, Tubbs told us where he saw him. Chap and I walked back one hundred yards, very quietly, and there he was.

I shot him well.

Tim and bushbuck

The Tiny Ten

Of all the diverse wildlife species in Africa, the animals that people are the least familiar with are the "Tiny Ten." These are ten species of very small antelope that live throughout Africa. They average two feet at the shoulder, and the males have straight horns about six inches long. There are two types: those who live in open savannas and those who live in deep forests or jungles. They are exclusively an "accidental encounter" creature that may result in a stalk, but there really isn't any tracking. The tiny antelope are seen and then shot if they don't dart away.

Tim and duiker

One day, as we were driving slowly along a dirt road, Chap stopped suddenly.

Chap whispered, "Duiker." Duiker are the most common of the Tiny Ten, with as many as twenty-two subspecies, with coloration running the gauntlet of tan, yellow, zebra-striped, and dark brown. This subspecies was the common duiker, with a tan color.

Chap and I got out of the truck, leaving the doors open so there would be no slamming sound. Tubbs stayed in the truck and handed my rifle to me. Chap and I slipped back down the dirt road, hugging the tree line. Chap slowly spread the sticks, then pointed towards the diminutive antelope forty yards into the dark mopane forest. The duiker stood still. I hit him on the shoulder, resulting in a beautiful mount.

Another of the Tiny Ten is the klipspringer, Boer for "rock jumper." While close to the duiker in size, they live in very different environments. The duiker lives in dark forests, and the klipspringer lives in kjopies.

When searching for "klippies," you have to examine the kjopie with binoculars. Like bighorn sheep and mountain goats, these small antelope are skilled at traversing boulders and steep cliffs. Klipspringers, however, are much smaller than either the sheep or the goat.

Tim and klipspringer

While driving between leopard hunts one day, Tubbs tapped the roof of the hunting truck to get Chap's attention. He had seen a klipspringer on the top of a kjopie a hundred yards ahead of us while it was crossing over to the other side of the kjopie. We stopped the truck, taking only the rifle and shooting sticks. Chap and I slowly, carefully walked around the kjopie, looking up for the klippie. We went into the cover of trees at the base of the hill. Chap and I glassed the kjopie from a hundred yards away.

"There. Good male, standing on a ledge below the female," Chap said.

Chap spread the sticks, pointing to a rocky ledge forty yards above the flat ground. I quickly got the female in the scope but couldn't see the male.

Chap whispered, "One yard below the female, one yard left."

I put the crosshairs on the female, dropped a yard, and went left a yard. I saw nothing.

"Do it again."

I did it again, but I still could not see the male.

"He's still there," Chap said. "Leave the scope on that spot."

I left the crosshairs on the spot, seemingly staring at a granite boulder. An ear flicked. Suddenly, the whole klippie sprang into my view, and I shot. He tumbled down the kjopie, coming to rest on the floor of the surrounding African bush. He's now a lovely little mount.

Eland

Completely opposite the Tiny Ten are eland, the world's biggest antelope. They stand five feet tall at the shoulder and weigh two thousand pounds. There are two species: the Livingstone eland and the Lord Derby eland. Zimbabwe has the Livingstone eland, which is slightly smaller than the West African Lord Derby eland. Although eland is a destination species and typically hunted by tracking, I experienced them in spot-and-stalk scenarios.

It was early evening, and Chap and I were driving back to camp. Suddenly, out of nowhere, a huge Livingstone eland jumped completely over the moving truck.

"Holy shit," we both expressed simultaneously.

Chap slammed on the brakes, and we jumped out. Tubbs threw my rifle at me. I cranked a round into the chamber, ensured the rifle's safety switch was on safe, and then ran after Chap, with Tubbs running after me. I had no intention of hunting an eland, but this opportunity was impossible to pass up.

We ran after it through the long grass and around the mopane trees. I was sure it would evade us. An eland can run twenty-five miles an hour for a short distance, but it can trot endlessly at fifteen miles an hour. It was late in the day, and I was tired. I wasn't sure how much longer I could run. As I ran into an open space, Chap had already set up the shooting sticks and was glassing an area about a hundred yards away. The eland was standing sideways and looking at us, giving me a perfect shoulder target. I shot, and it dropped behind dense bushes.

Seeing that I was completely gassed, Chap took my rifle and ran forward. I grabbed the sticks and staggered after Chap with Tubbs following me. When we caught up, Chap was sitting on the eland. It was huge.

Tim and Livingstone eland

As darkness fell, we loaded the eland into the truck, then headed back to camp in the dark of night. We dropped it at the skinning shed and retired to the warming fire with a glass of Windhoek.

Jackal

Jackals are omnivorous, dog-like animals similar in size to a German shepherd with a fox-like appearance. There are two species in sub-Saharan Africa: the black-backed jackal and the side-striped jackal. The jackal, for me, is a spot-and-stalk hunt. Tubbs or Japhet would spot a jackal, and we would jump out of the truck. We had to be fast, as jackals are skittish and will disappear when uncomfortable with their surroundings.

While I had seen jackals before, it was usually when I was hunting other animals, so we wouldn't stop to go after a jackal. On one occasion, however, we were heading back to camp when Tubbs tapped the top of the cab after sighting a black-backed jackal. We jumped out, and Chap set the shooting sticks. The jackal stood still, one hundred yards away, perfectly positioned for a shot, while looking in our direction. I set my .375 on the sticks, sighted carefully, squeezed the trigger, and missed him by a yard. While I was shocked at my ineptitude, the jackal didn't move an inch. With Chap, Tubbs, and Japhet chuckling behind me, I cranked another round into the chamber, took careful aim, and shot again. This time, I was successful. I bagged the feared African black-backed jackal.

He now lives with me as a full mount.

Warthog

Warthogs are a desired prey of leopards and, occasionally, hyenas and lions. For hunters, they have very attractive ivory from both their upper and lower tusks and are also loved as camp food.

I've only shot at a warthog once. We were slowly heading down the road towards camp late one evening when Chap suddenly pointed into the brush and said, "Female leopard."

As I turned my head to look, Chap slammed on the brakes, causing me to miss seeing the leopard.

"Warthog," he said, as the animal ran in front of the truck.

I quickly jumped out. Tubbs pulled me up onto the top of the truck, handing my rifle to me. Tubbs pointed into the growing dusk, about twenty yards away. Seen only through my light-gathering scope was a sitting warthog. I put the crosshairs on the middle of the body and shot.

"Hit it?" Tubbs asked.

I wasn't sure, as I was blinded by the flash of the .375.

We jumped down off the truck. Tubbs used a torch to follow a blood trail from the spot where it was sitting when I shot. Within ten yards we came upon a dead warthog. Chap grabbed him by his tusks and looked intently at the face.

"This isn't the one I saw," he said.

Tubbs and I looked at each other. Tubbs said, "New dead."

Chap paused for a second and said, "I know. Okay. Let's take him to the skinning shed."

We threw him into the back of the truck and headed out.

Chap was strangely quiet. We deposited the warthog into the skinning shed with the appropriate instructions (mount style, meat cuts) and returned to camp for our evening activities.

That night we had dinner with Chap's friend Pierre Hundermark, a tall, lean professional hunter who was visiting for the night. Suddenly, out of nowhere, Chap said emphatically, "That was not the warthog I saw."

Tim and the first warthog

We looked at Chap, not understanding what he meant.

"I wonder if there's another one lying out there," Chap said.

Pierre looked at me and asked, "You shot two?"

"I don't think so," I answered. "I only shot once."

We drank, ate, and went to bed, resolving to figure it out in the morning.

At five a.m., we gathered at the truck. As we loaded, Chap said, "We're going back. There's another dead warthog out there."

As we pulled up to the spot where I shot, Tubbs jumped out and ran to where the warthog was standing when I shot him.

Tim and Chap with the second warthog

In the growing light, Tubbs said, "There is another blood track."

We followed the second blood track. Thirty yards later we came to a dead warthog. Chap grabbed the tusks and looked at the face. "This is the one I saw," he said.

He laid the warthog down, turning him over. The warthog's groin and thighs were missing, having been eaten by a female leopard, probably the one Chap saw the night before.

His skull and tusks were undamaged, but the leopard had eaten the meat the warthog would have provided us. The interesting and obvious conclusion is that when I shot the warthog in the dark, I actually shot two at the same time. They were apparently standing side by side.

Killing two animals with one bullet is unusual, to say the least.

Waterbuck

Waterbucks are tall, handsome antelope, roughly the size of American elk. Their horns start backwards, then sweep forward. They make striking trophies. Although they are not a destination trophy, the method of hunting a waterbuck is the same as most African antelope—spot-and-stalk.

As attractive as they are, waterbucks have a strange, awful attribute. They secrete a repugnant, oily substance that coats their fur. Touching a waterbuck's coat reminds me of placing my hand on a plate of cooking oil. It's a nasty, messy sensation that smells very badly. When caping a waterbuck, the skinner must be careful not to let the hair and skin touch the meat. If the secreted oil of the hair gets on the meat, it will ruin its taste.

One evening, Chap, Tubbs, and I were cruising in a small boat along the shore of a tributary of the Zambezi. Tall, bare ironwood trees stood out of the river, which still remained from the flooding when the Kariba Dam was built in the late 1950s. Fish eagles, which are similar to bald eagles, sat on the top of the trees watching for their prey.

We were looking for a waterbuck. They need water consistently, probably more than any other antelope, so they normally stay close to waterways. We headed back to camp after Chap and Tubbs thought they had located where a bull waterbuck was living.

The next morning, we walked into the area where Chap and Tubbs expected to find the waterbuck. We walked slowly along the edge of a small forest next to the river and peered into the trees. Chap quietly spread the shooting sticks, onto which I placed my rifle. The waterbuck was forty yards away. He was standing quietly and was perfectly angled to me, which gave me a clean shoulder shot. He looked toward us, but he didn't see us. I centered the crosshairs squarely on his shoulder. He shifted slightly as I pulled the trigger.

When my .375 fired, the waterbuck leapt and took off running. Strangely, neither Chap, Tubbs, nor I saw which way he ran. He literally disappeared into the surrounding forest. We ran the forty yards to where he was standing when I shot. There was absolutely no blood.

"How was your shot? Did you hit him?" Chap asked.

Japhet with the waterbuck

"It was dead-on," I said. I can't often say that with certainty.

Chap pointed for Tubbs to go in one direction, while Chap and I went in the other direction. We went about fifty yards from where the waterbuck was shot and found him dead. We rolled him over to see the correctly placed entry wound; however, there was no exit wound.

The bullet strangely did not exit, so there was no blood. Fortunately, the skinners did a good job when removing the cape, as the meat was not spoiled.

Zebra

Zebras are not striped horses. They're mean, cannot be domesticated, and are a highly sought African trophy. I've brought five zebra skins back from Africa for various relatives.

Zebras are spot-and-stalk animals. Traveling around the hunting concession, Tubbs or Japhet would sometimes spot a dazzle of zebras. If I wanted to hunt one, we'd stop and unload and begin the difficult stalking; it's hard to get close to a zebra. A dazzle has too many eyes and too many ears. If I didn't want a zebra, we'd continue with what we were doing.

Once while we were driving in the Zambezi Valley, Tubbs spotted zebras in the distance. Chap and Tubbs determined that there was a good stallion in this dazzle. We unloaded and started the slow stalk to get within shooting distance.

Finally, we got within a hundred yards and crouched among the brush. Chap slowly set up the shooting sticks. I carefully set up my rifle and made sure that I didn't make any sudden movements. If I did, they would immediately notice us. Taking aim at the sergeant's stripes that formed on the front shoulder (an unfortunate species-wide birthmark), I fired a 300-grain bullet into the heart and lung of the stallion. He immediately dropped. The other zebras scattered; they didn't seem to care about the health of their former friend.

Tubbs, Tim, and a zebra stallion

We walked up, and I touched my rifle barrel to his eye to make sure he was dead. We took pictures, and then we winched him into the back of the hunting truck.

During an early zebra hunt, Chap and I went to Rossyln Safaris, a 32,000-acre hunting reserve just north of Bulawayo. Peter Johnson, an original Zimbabwe professional hunter (PH license #0001), bought the land in the late 1980s and developed an excellent hunting reserve. The reserve offers leopard, sable and many species of plains game, certainly including zebra.

Chap and I had dinner with Mr. Johnson on our first evening in camp. He told us stories of how he developed his reserve from a land with no animals into a reserve that is rich with game. Mr. Johnson is a man to be admired, an old Rhodesian big game hunter who has adapted to the new world.

Another time, while fruitlessly hunting impalas for a leopard bait, we came across a single zebra about eighty yards from us. A zebra, much bigger than an impala, can make four different leopard baits, so I positioned myself for a shot. Chap laid his hand across my rifle.

"Don't shoot," he said.

I waited. The zebra turned his head to look at us. I waited. The zebra turned away and walked into the brush.

"Why not?" I asked.

"Never shoot a single zebra," said Chap. "Without another to compare it to, you can't judge his age and size. He could have been a juvenile."

Moral of this story: never shoot juveniles. I guess.

Other Species

Lion

I've never hunted lions, and I probably never will.

The approach to lion hunting has changed in the last fifty years. Before the 1970s, hunters intentionally sought pride lions to hunt, specifically the lion who was the leader of a pride. This was before it was fully realized that when a pride loses its leader, the new pride lion kills all the cubs in order to induce the females into immediate estrus. Now, animal biologists prefer this pride ownership change to occur naturally. Today, the lion hunter's goal is to target lions that have completely black noses, which indicates that the lion is at least seven years old. Very few lions are pride lions past the age of five, so this practice ensures that lions are able to pass on their genetics for as long as they are capable of keeping their pride.

Hunting lions is similar to hunting leopards. The hunt starts by finding tracks of a lion and then a good lion tree nearby with thick branches five or ten feet from the ground. The hunter shoots bait for the hunt, but a leopard-appropriate impala is too small for a lion. Zebras are the most common animal shot for lion bait, but meat from any large animal will work: hippopotamus, giraffe, Cape buffalo. The bait is hung lower in the tree because the lion cannot climb like a leopard. The professional hunter, trackers, and client hunter then build a blind and wait. And wait. And wait.

Since the bait is hung lower, it may attract hyenas, leopards, or smaller cats. If these carnivores show up, the hunter does nothing, because if the lion is in the general vicinity, it will chase them off. If there is not one in the area, it doesn't matter, so the bait might as well feed other carnivores.

There is, however, an additional method for hunting lions: calling them in. At dusk, the professional hunter sets up a loudspeaker attached to an audio player. He broadcasts the sound of a lion moaning into the evening air. Lions are very competitive, so if one hears another lion in his territory, he will rush to the sound, looking to fight his challenger.

The professional hunter and his client will be in a typically constructed blind, waiting for the jealous lion to show up for a showdown with the interloper. When the lion appears, the hunters turn lights on and immediately make a shoot or no-shoot decision, based on guessing the age of the lion.

I've been told of two humorous situations which happened in a lion blind.

The first: when a professional hunter and his client were sitting in a lion blind, staring at the lion bait, a lion paw suddenly swept under the bottom of the blind.

Apparently a lion came from the side of the blind to the front, unseen by the professional hunter and the client. Lions, like all cats, can be curious. This lion didn't realize that the blind was occupied by living meat. It just swept under the blind, then walked away from the startled hunters.

The second: a professional hunter and his client were sitting in a blind, watching the bait. The professional hunter suddenly had a strange feeling; he turned around and saw an adult lioness sitting, staring at the hunters. The professional hunter said nothing, not even reaching for his rifle. He just kept watching the lioness. After another minute, the lioness stood and wandered away. The professional hunter waited several minutes before telling his client what had happened. His client was amazed. And greatly relieved.

I hadn't seen lions in the wild until one day when Chap, Tubbs, and I were following elephant tracks that took us past a little pond. The elephant had not stopped to drink, so we kept going. Eventually, Tubbs realized we were not getting any closer to the elephant, so we turned back.

As we approached the little pond on the return, we saw a lioness sitting on the shore, staring at us. We stopped to watch her from about twenty yards. After a few minutes, she laid down and started lapping water, never taking her eyes off us. As we stood there, I realized Chap and Tubbs weren't looking at her; they were scanning the surrounding area looking for the male lion, who was sure to be there.

Suddenly, Tubbs pointed. Sitting in a sphinx position, the lion was forty yards away from us. He was in a patch of wispy grass the color of his tawny coat, watching us from under the shade of the tree line. It would have been impossible for me to see the lion without Chap and Tubbs pointing him out. What a beautiful creature, I thought, as he stared at us with his piercing yellow eyes.

The lion stood up, still staring at us. He slowly walked towards us and then abruptly broke out into a sprint, straight for us. I froze with terror. He suddenly pulled up twenty yards short of us. He stood still, stared at us, and then turned and trotted away. Followed by the lioness, he disappeared into the bush. During the charge, I noticed that neither Chap nor Tubbs moved.

Lioness at the pond

I turned to Chap. "You knew he wasn't charging?" I stuttered.

"Ya. No charge," he answered as he walked away, demonstrating his field knowledge gained through years of African hunting. And we left.

Other than hearing lions moan in the distance over a campfire, that's my only lion experience in Africa, and it's more than enough.

Baboon

Baboons are everywhere. A gathering of baboons is called a troop. They form into big troops, medium troops, and small troops. Troops are everywhere. While not the most feared, baboons are probably the most disliked animal in Africa. On top of that, their excrement smells horrible.

Baboons hang around the villages. While I've never heard of people being harmed by one, I sure wouldn't want them around small children.

Baboons are actually fun to watch. When we approached a troop, all of the younger baboons moved to the back. The dominant male and his pals moved to the front and emitted stark low-pitched barks. Younger baboons have the same bark, except with a higher, squeakier pitch.

Baboons are fun to harass. In the evening, troops will climb tall palm trees and gather in the fronds as protection from leopards. Occasionally, while driving back to the camp after a hard hunt, Chap will turn off his lights and creep towards a palm tree. At the last second, he will turn on his lights, slam into the tree, and honk his horn. The baboons will scream and jump from the tree, landing on the ground and scattering into the darkness.

Other than strange mounts or bait for leopards and hyenas, there's not much interest in baboons on an African safari.

The local villagers would occasionally run to the truck and ask us to, "Come kill baboon. Come kill baboon." We normally didn't.

Crocodile

I've never hunted the two most commonly hunted water animals that live in the rivers, ponds, and streams of Zimbabwe: hippos and crocs. Both are exceedingly dangerous animals.

Crocodiles will grab their prey—impala, zebra, wildebeest, human—drag it into the water, go into a death roll, and begin tearing meat from their victim. Crocs can't chew their food; they can only swallow. I don't hunt them for two rational reasons: I don't shoot well enough to ensure a death shot, and crocodiles terrify me.

Crocodiles are usually baited on the sandy shore of a river. The meat is anchored with a chain that is connected to a rod driven deep into the sand. When an appropriately sized croc (longer than twelve feet) comes to the bait, the hunter shoots at its golf ball-sized brain from at least forty yards away.

Since I can't hit a golf ball from forty yards, there's no point for me to hunt crocodiles.

Hippopotamus

Hippopotamuses, the third largest land mammal in the world, behind the elephant and the rhino, are very dangerous to humans. In the daylight, they will capsize small boats and crush their victims with their huge mouths.

At night, they are even more dangerous. Hippos leave their water habitat to graze grass, often wandering miles from the river. If a local gets between the grazing hippo and the river, the hippo will crush the offending villager. Hippos, in fact, are thought to kill the most people in Africa.

I don't hunt hippos for the same reason I don't hunt crocs: I'm not a good enough shot, and I don't want to be near the water's edge.

Hippos are hunted during the day. This is done by quietly approaching the river and looking for a pod of them in the water. Once located, the professional hunter will select one based on its size and sex. Since only its ears and eyes are visible while it's in the water, this is a pretty complicated thing to do. The professional hunter will point out the large bull hippo to kill, and the client will aim at its tennis ball-sized brain gently bobbing in the water. The hippo, if killed, will sink into the river. After a few hours, the gasses in the dead hippo will float the huge beast. The hunting crew then attaches a rope and drags it to shore, where it is cut for eating meat, skin, tusks, lion bait, or other desired trophies. The assumption is that the client can hit a bobbing tennis ball-sized brain at eighty yards. If you don't brain-shoot the hippo, then you end up paying a lot of money for the pleasure of missing a target. Since I can't hit a bobbing tennis ball at eighty yards, I don't hunt hippos.

Although I had no intention of hunting hippos, I did have several interesting encounters with them.

Chap and I were in camp one day when we got the word that a local village was having a hippo problem. Chap, in his gracious and inclusive way, asked me if I'd like to hunt the PAC hippo with him.

We jumped into the hunting truck and took off for the village. Perhaps it was the excitement and the danger, but I thought that this might give me the confidence to trophy hunt a hippo. The hippo-threatened village was pretty far away; it took about an hour to get there. As we crested the hill overlooking the village next to the river, we saw that the adjacent fields were plowed, and green vegetables were starting to grow. The village women were in the fields planting and weeding. If the hippo had settled into the area near the village, the villagers would be in constant danger. We stopped short of the village. Tubbs, our Ndebele negotiator, headed down to see the village elders.

After thirty minutes, Tubbs returned to the truck, spoke to Chap in Ndebele, and climbed up into the back. Chap laughed as he started the truck. "That hippo is in the middle of acres of reeds," he said. "We're not going in there." Although disappointed, I certainly wasn't going to hunt a rogue hippo in chest-deep water in a field of reeds with a visibility of three yards. So, we left. A few days later, Ian Wakefield, the camp apprentice, killed the hippo. I'm just sorry it wasn't me.

Another time, we were wandering through a forest without much underbrush, almost like one of the German forests where all the underbrush is removed. We came upon a circular pond, about fifty yards in diameter. In the middle of the pond floated a large bull hippo. I wasn't hunting hippos, but we stopped at the side of the pond to observe. He started drifting towards us. We moved to another vantage point to watch him. He altered his direction towards us. We moved again, and he began drifting towards us, again, although he was drifting faster. We moved again, and the hippo moved towards us, again, but at an even faster pace.

Chap said, "It's time to leave. We don't want a confrontation with this monster."

Another hippo story: on a waterbuck hunt, we lost his tracks, so we went to a nearby bluff to rest.

The bluff was about a hundred feet above a small, slowly flowing river with a long flat plain of bush and mopane trees on the other side, seemingly to the horizon. I looked into the distant bush for any buffalo, zebra or giraffe, but I saw none. I imagined walking across the plain, realizing that in Africa, we could come across anything. Or nothing.

In the river below us was a cow hippopotamus and her calf. The calf was swimming around his mother, while she was very still, allowing her baby to exercise in the calm water with no other hippos around to bother them.

We sat, recovering our strength from the waterbuck hunt, drinking water, and just watched the hippos float alone in the river. Suddenly, Tubbs stood, pointed into the distance, and spoke to Chap in Ndebele. Chap stood, took out his binoculars, and gazed in the direction Tubbs pointed for several minutes.

I waited while Chap looked, then I asked what it was about.

"Tubbs sees a poacher," Chap told me.

"Any idea what he is poaching? Elephant?"

"No, one man doesn't poach elephant. He was probably a bush poacher, checking his snares."

We finished resting, threw some small rocks at the hippos, which didn't come close, and resumed hunting.

Cheetah

Cheetahs are large cats, weighing anywhere from ninety to one hundred fifty pounds. They are mostly noted for their speed. Cheetahs are considered the fastest land mammal on earth, reaching seventy MPH for up to one hundred yards. After cheetahs kill their prey, they have to lie across it until they catch their breath. This is a problem because the cheetah cannot defend its prize; if a hyena or a lion shows up, the cheetah slinks away, having lost its dinner to a bigger, more aggressive carnivore.

Cheetahs are appropriately protected in Zimbabwe. However, I believe they will eventually be extinct in the wild because they require open ground to run down their prey. In Zimbabwe and other African countries, as the human population expands, open savanna is converted to farmland, which is not conducive to the antelope herds that the cheetahs hunt. Cheetahs are very specialized cats and cannot adapt to their environment like leopards or American coyotes can. Eventually, I believe, cheetahs will only be seen in zoos.

Wild Dogs

Another interesting carnivore in Zimbabwe is the African wild dog, also known as the painted dog or the Cape hunting dog. They are considered the most effective pack hunters in Africa. Typically, a pack will chase an impala herd until a single impala shows weakness, at which point the entire pack will focus on the single impala. The pack will run it down and begin eating the impala while it's still alive. Before long, the impala is completely gone. The pack will go rest in the shade, having eaten their fill for the day. Professional hunters don't like wild dogs, probably for the same reason North American outfitters don't like wolves. Both species reduce the available trophy animals their clients want to hunt.

Several times Chap and I drove past dog packs who were resting after a successful hunt. We stopped to observe the pack; they raised their heads, looked at us for several seconds, then flopped their heads back down. The wild dogs are endangered due to cross breeding with domestic dogs and catching the diseases of domestic dogs, including rabies. Wild dogs, therefore, are protected and cannot be hunted.

Fishing

Occasionally there were breaks in my safari, either changing locations after a successful hunt for a destination animal or simply because we wanted a break. We sometimes fished during these breaks. Chap is one of Zimbabwe's greatest fishermen. If he could, I suspect he would be a professional fisherman instead of a professional hunter. He belongs to all the fishing clubs in Bulawayo, if not Zimbabwe. Many times, when he and I were driving from one place in Zimbabwe to another, Chap honked his horn at the oncoming truck of a fellow fisherman.

Since I am deathly afraid of crocodiles, it's hard for me to approach the shore of a stream or pond in Africa. I can literally imagine a huge croc, laying in ambush, ready to grab and drag me under, never to be seen again. Smooth-talking Chap, however, was able to convince me to fish now and then.

One time, Chap, Mike, and I took a small boat from our hunting camp to the shore of a fishing camp. While we were fishing there, Mike caught a tigerfish, which is probably the most interesting fish in southern Africa. Tigerfish resemble striped bass, grow up to three feet long, and have the biggest, sharpest teeth imaginable. Mike caught one that was about fourteen inches long. It was fascinating to see but not exactly a prize.

More memorably, Mike caught a big tilapia. This tilapia was unlike the small, skinny, white fish bought in American grocery stores. This one was eighteen inches long, ten inches tall, and four inches thick. We took it back to our camp to have the camp cook prepare it. It was the best tasting fish I have ever eaten.

Mike with a small tigerfish

Another fishing experience was at a hunting camp located on the Ume River, a tributary of Lake Kariba in northern Zimbabwe. We took a pontoon boat into the channel, specifically looking for vundu catfish. Vundu can reach five feet long and weigh a hundred and twenty pounds. They are fairly easy to hook but are very hard to pull in. In this situation, we brought a few back for the staff, but we mostly caught and released them.

As we were sitting on the pontoon boat in the Ume, I saw two things you would not normally see while fishing in the Lake of the Ozarks. The first was a small herd of elephants that had come out of the brush to drink along a shoreline about two hundred yards from us. We watched them a while, but they didn't pay any attention to us. After a while, having satisfied their thirst, they turned and disappeared into the bush.

The second was a crocodile that cruised past us at about one hundred yards away. We could only imagine what the croc was doing, or where it was going, as they normally stay along the shoreline, waiting for some poor animal to venture too close. Being terrified of crocs, I didn't suggest we motor over to ask what it's intentions were.

Egyptian Geese

My first, and last, actual bird hunt involved an Egyptian goose, a bird from the Nile Valley and southern Africa which can weigh up to five pounds. Mike, Tubbs, Japhet, and I were driving back to the hunting camp one day when Tubbs tapped on the roof of the truck cab. Mike leaned out, listened to Tubbs, and abruptly pulled over. Turning to me, he asked, "Do you want to hunt an Egyptian goose?"

"What?" I responded, not quite understanding what was happening.

"We just passed a couple on the ground. The boys want one for dinner. I've got a .22 mag you can use."

Mike got out of the hunting truck, reached behind the cab, and pulled out a .22 magnum rifle. Handing it to me, Mike pointed into the bush. He leaned against the truck, obviously not going anywhere, leaving the heavy lifting to me. Tubbs tugged on my shirt, and we started off into the bush. Twenty-five yards from the truck, we came upon a little pond with three Egyptian geese standing on the other side, probably forty yards away. Tubbs stepped behind me. It was time for me to learn how to shoot Mike's rifle.

Tim with an Egyptian goose for tracker's dinner

I squatted against an old tree, aimed into the middle of the goose, and fired. It flopped around for a few seconds, then settled down. Tubbs ran around the little pond, picked up the goose by the legs, and ran back to the truck. I gave the rifle back to Mike, proud that I added to the tracker's dinner in a meaningful way.

Vultures

While driving during an elephant hunt, Tubbs saw a bunch of vultures on the ground. We had to investigate; who knew what we'd find? We climbed out of, and off, the truck. Chap and I took our rifles because, after all, we were in Africa, and we could come across anything at any time, particularly when investigating a carcass. All carnivores love a free meal.

Tubbs started walking towards the vultures, with Japhet, Chap, and me following. About forty yards away we saw a great tumble of vultures climbing over each other, obviously tearing at something. As we got closer, the vultures began to notice us. When we were within fifteen yards, the vultures began taking off, each in its own direction. I realized, almost too late to act, that a vulture was coming straight towards me. At the last second, I ducked, avoiding the substantive part of the vulture, but its wing brushed softly against my face. After I recovered from the physical assault by the bird, we walked up to find a pitiful little impala whose carcass was feeding a dozen or so vultures.

The guys studied the impala but could not find any reason for its death. The only wounds on its body were caused by the hooked beaks of the carnivorous vultures.

Red-billed Quelea

Once, while hunting buffalo, we came upon a bare, leafless tree heavy with thousands of small birds. As we approached the tree, all the quelea birds simultaneously took to the air, keeping a tight formation. They created the appearance of a formless, shifting black cloud. After a dozen seconds, the black cloud settled back onto the tree.

Quelea are small, sparrow-like birds. They gather in huge groups and are thought of by farmers as locusts, as they will settle on fields of grain and strip the field bare in no time.

They are considered the most numerous undomesticated birds on earth and are a wonder to watch when the entire colony takes to the air.

Guineafowl

Guineafowl is another bird you cannot avoid seeing in Africa. They are everywhere in the bush. Although they can fly, they are usually seen on the ground in large groups.

As we drove along a rough road in the bush, guineafowl would come out and start running ahead of our hunting truck. Only when we eventually caught up would they dash into the bush or into the air, narrowly avoiding being run over.

On one drive, we had dozens of guineafowls running ahead of us when Tubbs leaned over to talk with Chap. Suddenly, Chap accelerated, running above several before they had a chance to take off. Chap quickly stopped, allowing Tubbs and Japhet to jump out and run back to the disheveled guineafowl. The trackers grabbed them, broke their necks, and brought back six or eight for their well-deserved dinner.

Later I asked Chap about how good guineafowl is to eat. Chap said, "Fill a big pot with water, add guineafowl meat, potatoes, onions, and a brick, and bring to a boil. After one hour, throw the guineafowl meat away, and eat the brick."

I never tried guineafowl. I wish I had.

Secretary Bird

Although I've only seen one, I've given the secretary bird a spot in my African memoirs because it's such a striking bird. When standing, they reach five feet tall, although they only weigh eleven or twelve pounds. We were driving down a dirt road when Chap slowed down, pointed ahead, and said, "There's a secretary bird."

Looking forward, I saw a tall, gangly bird running down the road ahead of us, awkwardly advancing on one leg, then the other. As we slowed down, staying fifteen yards behind the bird, it began flapping its wings as it ran. Slowly, it pulled itself into the air, eventually disappearing into the distance.

Martial Eagle

Like the secretary bird, I've only seen one martial eagle. We were driving in the bush when suddenly, just in front of us, a huge bird suddenly took flight. Chap slowed down and pointed out a little steenbok laying on the ground, half eaten. We had startled a martial eagle from its midday meal. A martial eagle, indigenous to sub-Saharan Africa, is a large and powerful eagle. It is the apex predator of the avian world in Africa, capable of killing and eating many small herbivores, such as hare, hyrax, and antelope. Chap told me that it has long talons, and, if it doesn't kill its prey with the initial dive, will lift its prey into the air to drop it repeatedly, until dead.

Unfortunately, martial eagles are becoming endangered, as sustenance farmers shoot or poison the large, aggressive eagle to protect their small livestock, such as lambs, chickens, piglets, and other species.

Yellow-billed Hornbill

And finally, my favorite bird in Africa. Yellow-billed hornbills are numerous, beautiful, and can dart around tree branches with amazing dexterity. As we drove through the hunting concession, I watched for them in the woodland, as they were amazing fliers, almost magically flying through the trees, angling, darting, and flitting through the branches and leaves, touching nothing.

In a discussion with Cuan Meredith, I asked if I could have one taxidermed to stand on a mount or a wooden branch mounted in my house in America. He told me that the yellow-billed hornbill was not on the "ship to America" list, so he could not mount one for me.

I later lamented over dinner with Chap and a fellow who said he was a Zimbabwean naturalist about not being able to take a mounted yellow-billed hornbill to America. The expert, to Chap's and my surprise, said that the yellow-billed hornbill was endangered. I responded that they were as common here as sparrows or robins are in America.

"No, no. They are endangered," he insisted.

Chap and I shifted the conversation to some other topic. We later agreed that the gentleman, however well-meaning he was, apparently never spent any time in Zimbabwe's wilderness.

Other Stories

My Taxidermist

The taxidermy company that I have used, Trophy Consultants International (TCI), is located in Bulawayo. TCI is owned by Cuan Meredith, a young, white Zimbabwean. Whenever I was in Bulawayo, I always visited his factory.

His front office and show room is a wondrous place full of shoulder mounts, including one of an elephant, and rows of purses, bags, and luggage made from animal skins. The expansive factory floor houses dozens of artisans working on dozens of animals in various stages of taxidermy. Whenever we drop in, we are able to admire an artist carefully painting the face of a baboon or stitching the hide of an impala skin together around an "impala form." These forms are the shape of the specific animal being taxidermed. The animal's tanned skin covers the form. Piles of skins from all the different animals of Zimbabwe are stacked on the floor. These skins do not belong to other hunters; instead, they're used by TCI in various ways, like bags, purses, and rugs.

We usually finish up sipping beers in Cuan's office, discussing how I want my trophies to look when they are finished.

Also, Cuan Meredith also owns a large houseboat capable of sleeping six individuals. The boat, *River God*, takes fishermen and tourists up and down the Zambezi both fishing for tigerfish and sightseeing various wildlife that can be seen from the boat.

Public Transportation in the Bush

One evening, I was being driven from one camp to another with Zimbabwe professional hunter, Boet van Arde. As we neared my hunting camp, we suddenly had to dodge a very large suitcase laying in the middle of the dirt road. Boet stopped immediately. We all got out and went back to the suitcase. The suitcase, laying open, had been packed, in fact overpacked, with clothes, bags of rice, and an unidentifiable number of personal items, for children as well as adults.

Boet and his trackers tried to put the suitcase back together, but the hinges were broken, and the suitcase had been packed absolutely full, so it was impossible to be repacked. We put the open suitcase, with the contents piled on top, in the back of Boet's truck.

As we started up again, Boet believed the suitcase was packed on top of a bus, and had fallen off. We were going to try to catch up with the bus to return the suitcase and contents.

After a short while, we caught up to the bus. It had pulled over into a dimly lit small village. The bus had emptied, and dozens of men and women crowded around two men who were shouting and shoving each other.

Boet pulled up, honking his horn. He jumped out, and talked to the two men, the owner of the suitcase and the bus driver, who were on the verge of fighting. Boet's trackers grabbed the suitcase and its contents, and ran around to where the bus was stopped.

The men stopped fighting, and a woman, the suitcase owner, began repacking the suitcase. The men calmed down and spoke to Boet, shaking his hand.

We returned to Boet's truck and resumed travelling to my hunting camp. Boet told me that the bus ran once every day or two, and was always terribly packed. Luggage went on top, and which apparently wasn't always secure... as we saw.

Matobo National Park

Matobo National Park is just south of Bulawayo in southwest Zimbabwe. It is an animal reserve that has a number of white and black rhinoceroses that are protected by a strong ranger presence. Unfortunately, in my one trip through the park, I saw no rhinos.

Tim at Cecil Rhodes' gravesite

My purpose for being there, however, was to visit the gravesite of Cecil John Rhodes, the noted British colonialist and expansionist who became fabulously wealthy from the South African diamond fields in the 1880s and 1890s. His nationalistic goal was to build railroad tracks from Cape Town to Cairo, making all of Africa a

British colony. As part of his plan, he took Zimbabwe (then Southern Rhodesia) as his own.

Before he died in 1902, he had told his government leaders that he wanted to be buried in the Matobo Hills. His gravesite is in a spectacular place, high in the boulders of Matobo. Although it is only a minor tourist attraction, Cecil Rhodes is viewed as an embarrassment to the Zimbabwean government, which doesn't want to be reminded of its history of white rule.

Chipangali Wildlife Orphanage

Just south of Bulawayo is a strange, small, zoo-like facility where injured wild animals are brought for rehab. Chap and I visited the Wildlife Orphanage while we were in Bulawayo between hunting locations.

It's a comfortable little place shaded by leafy trees along broad walking paths, sided by benches to sit and have an ice cream. The leopard cages, for instance, are large, soil bottomed, and full of many different types of plants to ensure that the cats are as comfortable as possible, which is considerably better than many Western zoos. There are cages of baboons and vervet monkeys, ponds with crocs, and other enclosures with various wildlife. There are often a sizeable number of people, including many children, strolling around like at any zoo.

One notable caged enclosure, however, was strange. During our visit, Chap and I walked up to a large enclosure that was void of animals. Scattered around were large tree trunks lying on the ground with thick, bare branches. The ground was hard-packed dirt. Several workers entered the cage, each carrying huge slabs of meat, which Chap thought was donkey meat.

The workers draped the meat slabs on the thick branches around the enclosure. After six slabs of meat were draped across the wood, the workers left. Several minutes later, a gate was opened, and six adult lions charged into the enclosure. Each, as if carefully trained, went to a separate log for his meat. There was no growling, snarling, or fighting. Each lion went to his seemingly pre-planned place.

Two things stood out. First, they were young adults, as indicated by their primarily pink noses. As lions age, their noses turn black. By the time lions are five or six years old, their noses are completely black. I also noticed that these lions were not affected by human presence. Wild lions are very skittish around humans. Since they were young and accustomed to humans, the implication was that they were captivity--bred lions. There are only two purposes for captivity-bred lions: zoos or "canned hunting," the latter of which is common in South Africa. Zoos only have captivity-bred lions. With canned hunting, however, captivity-bred lions are put into fenced areas containing prey for the lion to kill and eat. Once the lion has been left alone for a month in the enclosure, clients, paying enormous amounts of money, can enter the enclosure to hunt it, with almost no chance of failure.

We didn't ask. We just watched as the lions locked their golden eyes on us and devoured their slabs of donkey meat.

Russian Hunters

Africa is mostly hunted by Americans, but other nationalities hunt in Africa as well. Seventy percent of Chap's clients are American, fifteen percent are Russian, and fifteen percent are Spanish. While I've only encountered a few fellow hunters in Africa, the most humorous situation I've had was with a Russian couple.

One night I was preparing for the next day's trip back to America. The airstrip was about a three-hour drive from our camp. Chap suggested we spend the evening in another camp, which was only a thirty-minute drive from the airstrip.

Chap and I pulled into the other camp that evening. There was a Russian hunter and his wife in the camp who were being guided on an elephant hunt by Alan Moodie, a Zimbabwean professional hunter. They had already eaten dinner, so Chap and I ate quickly and joined them at the fire pit as evening settled over us.

After a few minutes, the Russian hunter looked at me intently. He beat his fist onto his chest and growled, "Me four seventy." Not understanding what he said, I just looked back at him and said nothing.

"Me four seventy," he said again. "You?"

Aha. I caught on. He was saying he used a .470 nitro express double rifle.

I replied, "I have a .375 Holland and Holland."

He pounded his chest again and grunted with satisfaction, "Four seventy."

I guess he was equating his masculinity with the caliber of the rifle he used, which, in his mind, made him bigger and better than me. I said nothing more; I just thought he was a narcissistic ass.

We sat around the fire and drank beer. Not much else was said until Alan stood and stretched.

"Five a.m. wake-up?" Alan asked the Russian couple.

"No, no, no, no," the Russian woman responded. It turned out the woman could speak English, but the husband could not, except for describing his rifle caliber.

This set Alan back. "Five a.m. for hunting?" he asked again.

"No, no, no, no," was the response.

There was a notable pause from Alan. "Then when do you want to hunt?"

Chap and I stood up to leave for our huts. There was nothing we could add to this conversation.

We woke up the next morning around six, ate breakfast, and left for the airstrip. Nobody else was around the camp. Shortly after we left, while we were driving out of the concession, Alan contacted Chap by truck-to-truck radio while driving around with his tracker, looking for elephants. Alan's client had stayed at the fire pit deep into the night, drinking. The Russian's wife had told Alan to lock the liquor up for the night. He had. What Alan didn't do was lock the beer away. During the night, Mr. Four Seventy drank a case of beer. Consequently, neither he nor his wife got up to hunt that morning.

Alan asked Chap to watch for elephants on our drive to the airstrip. We did, in fact, see a mediocre elephant, as defined by his tusk size. We stopped, tied toilet paper to a tree, and reported the location to Alan.

Alan eventually went hunting without the Russian couple, shot an elephant with small tusks, returned to camp to retrieve the Russians, and took them to the dead elephant for pictures. The Russians were ecstatic.

Russians. Strange hunters.

The Great Zimbabwe

The Great Zimbabwe is a medieval city that flourished from the eleventh century through the fifteenth century in the south-central hills of Zimbabwe. It was a royal palace for the regional monarchs. The most interesting aspect about Great Zimbabwe, other than its sprawling 1,800-acre size, is that it was constructed with stone but without mortar. Eventually, it was abandoned and left to itself. The Portuguese were the first to write about Great Zimbabwe in 1531, but the first confirming visits by Europeans didn't come until 1871.

The white Rhodesian government, in an act of amazing racism, stated that the Great Zimbabwe couldn't have been built by the indigenous people. It was too spectacular, and the indigenous people, the Shona or Ndebele, weren't smart enough to build it. Regardless of who built it (and indigenous people DID build it), the Great Zimbabwe was a critical element in the history of southern Africa; it was the crossroads of trade from central Africa to Zanzibar.

Japhet (L) and Tubbs exploring Great Zimbabwe

In a scheduled break while on a hunt with Chap, Tubbs, and Japhet, I suggested we visit the Great Zimbabwe. To my surprise, they had never been there. So, we took off for a visit.

A humorous aspect of our trip was that we couldn't find the Great Zimbabwe. Chap knew the general direction, but we went past the unmarked cut-off and went into the town past it. We asked people in the town where it was, and they told us to go back about seven or eight miles and turn left. Eventually, we got there.

It was a beautiful park setting, with a nice museum that explained the growth of the Great Zimbabwe and the cultural implications to this area and southern Africa.

I went into the museum and met the curator, a black Zimbabwean, who was dressed in a dark suit and tie, which is unusual in Zimbabwe. As I turned to the first exhibit, a diorama, he joined me. I asked about the exhibit. He gladly stepped up and led me around. He explained the people, the cultures, the structures, and the history of the Great Zimbabwe. The hour that I spent there was fascinating. The curator had been educated in Zimbabwe, completed additional schooling overseas, and returned to research the ancient cultures of Zimbabwe. When finished, I climbed the various structures of the Great Zimbabwe with Chap, Japhet, and Tubbs, including toiling up winding staircases to the top of the Great Zimbabwe, where there was a royal residence.

I am now even more impressed with Zimbabwe. I just wish they would put direction signs up.

Elephant Stories

During my time hunting elephants, I was fortunate to observe two interesting strings of elephant herds.

The first sighting occurred in Hwange National Park, while Chap and I were staying at the Nehimba to cure myself of jet lag. We drove around the park just observing the wildlife. We stopped as a herd of elephants passed in front of us. Chap turned off the jeep engine, and we watched the elephants cross over the rough dirt road about twenty yards in front of us. They all crossed in single file—bulls, cows, young, old—occasionally glancing at us.

After twenty or twenty-five elephants passed in front of us, we thought they were all gone. Chap started the jeep but then suddenly turned it off. An older female came out of the bush, walking very slowly. Behind her, a very young elephant, maybe a month old, followed, limping awkwardly, staggering behind its mother. The mother and her baby finally crossed the road and continued following the herd into the bush.

"That calf is really injured," I noted to Chap.

"Yeah, it happens," Chap replied. "It either fell badly when it was born, or an older elephant accidentally stepped on it."

"Damn, what will happen to it?" I asked.

"It'll be killed eventually. Lions will take it."

In a less depressing story, Chap and I were elephant hunting once in the Ngamo teak forest. As dusk approached, we began walking towards the place for Japhet to pick us up. Suddenly, out of the growing darkness, a stream of elephants emerged from the dense bush and passed within fifty yards in front of us. It was a single line of twenty elephants, all bulls, traveling into the distant wilderness.

Amazingly, they were in order of size. The biggest was first, and the smaller trailed behind. Occasionally, two of the smaller bulls would turn around and head butt each other in juvenile fighting. After fifteen or twenty seconds, the two young bulls would break off the mock fight and rush to rejoin their place in the elephant string.

We watched for ten minutes as the elephant parade headed into the darkening bush. We then resumed our trip back to the hunting camp.

Bubi River Hotel & Bar

In southern Zimbabwe, when we realized we couldn't hunt female impalas at the concession where we had hunted my nyala, Chap, the tracking team, and I headed for a second hunting concession. Since animals are tightly regulated in the safari concessions, it's not unusual for a species to fall off the "can hunt" list.

While driving in the early afternoon, we came upon the Bubi River Hotel & Bar, a watering hole that Chap frequented. The Bubi River

Hotel & Bar was a way station for Southern Rhodesians, now Zimbabweans, traveling to and from Johannesburg, South Africa.

We pulled into the parking lot of hard-packed ground with ample leafy trees to provide protection from the equatorial sun. Tubbs and Japhet stretched out in the shade for an afternoon nap, while Chap and I went into the bar for a cool beer.

Inside the air-conditioned room was an old-fashioned mahogany bar, scarred with generations of use, but kept shiny and clean, with an old lion shoulder mount peering down at those who sat in its shadow. We ordered a couple of Zambezi Lagers, the national beer of Zimbabwe. We slowly sipped our lagers and discussed local hunting with the barman. After we finished our second Zambezi Lager, we went back to the safari truck, woke up Tubbs and Japhet, and resumed our trip to the second hunting concession.

Poaching

There are generally two types of poaching: sustenance poaching and commercial poaching. Sustenance poaching is when the indigenous people illegally kill animals for food. A sad situation in Zimbabwe is that the citizens are not allowed to hunt local animals. Instead, they will set snares to capture impalas, duikers, or other small antelope. Unfortunately, they will occasionally snare carnivores (lions, leopards, and other cats) or even, in one situation I discussed earlier, elephants. Sustenance poaching is poaching, but, in light of the difficult economic situation in Zimbabwe, I cannot criticize this activity.

Commercial poaching is when animals are illegally killed for body parts rather than meat. In Africa, rhinoceroses and elephants are popular targets for their horns and tusks, respectively. The horns or the tusks are taken from the illegally killed rhino or elephant and shipped to the country funding the process. The horns or tusks are usually taken specifically for the markets in China and Viet Nam.

Is there a difference in poaching an elephant for its tusks and a client hunter hunting an elephant for its tusks? Absolutely. The trophy hunter is regulated by country wildlife groups, non-government organizations (NGOs), and US hunting organizations that take population and replacement rate of the species into consideration. Only a certain number, sex, or age of a species may be hunted. Legal hunting helps species continue to exist in the wild. With client hunting, significant fees are paid to the country and local governments. The proceeds either help manage the hunting environment or help the community fund schools, hospitals, or other needed infrastructures.

Poachers have no such considerations, as any sex or age is killed. They will kill a cow elephant with small tusks and a calf, leaving her calf with absolutely no chance to live. The tusks are hacked out of the dead cow's face, while the calf runs around wildly. The tusks are smuggled out of the country with no consideration of the continuation of the species or financial consideration for the community. Without a mother, the calf will die.

The rhino situation is identical to the elephant one but with a slight, interesting difference. At one time, country rhino managers and environmentalists decided that rhinos would be spared from poachers by cutting off their horns. This would render them useless to poachers. What was not considered, however, was that the poachers, having tracked down a hornless rhino, would kill it so they wouldn't waste their time by tracking down the same hornless rhino a second time. This is a perfect example of the "unintended consequences" of an otherwise humane wildlife act.

Both animal species are greatly endangered by commercial poaching. Controlled, managed trophy hunting can help keep both animals off the endangered list. More importantly, African countries need to patrol the bush where poachers kill their prey and manage the ports from where illegally poached tusks and rhino horns are shipped.

Malaria

Malaria is a terrible disease in Africa. Ninety percent of malaria deaths in the world occur in southern Africa, with an estimated 500,000 in 2017. As I noted earlier, everybody visiting southern Africa must take malaria pills.

There are many available, effective malaria pills, but each has side effects. The most interesting side effect I've read about is "bad dreams." Since I didn't want to have bad dreams while hunting dangerous game, I selected another anti-malarial medicine.

One time I probably didn't pay enough attention to the side effect of the pills I took to Africa. I always took my malaria pill when I got out of bed. Early in a hunt, we had breakfast at the normal time of five a.m. After eating, while carrying my rifle and gear to the truck, I suddenly bent over and projectile vomited. As I straightened up, Chap, Thabani, Japhet, and the ranger were staring at me. I realized that, despite what had happened in the last thirty seconds, I felt fine. After rinsing my mouth with water, we started the hunt.

The next morning, the same thing happened. I took my malaria pill as soon as I woke up. After I ate my eggs, bacon, and fruit, I walked to the truck, bent over, and projectile vomited. Again, after cleaning up my mouth, I was fine. Chap and I discussed my immediately vomiting after eating and decided that I had to do something different because not taking the pills wasn't an option.

The next morning, I woke at three a.m. and took my malaria pill. After breakfast two hours later, I was fine. I had found the solution: take my malaria pill two hours before eating.

Another time I was involved in a situation which was an interesting combination of malaria prevention and poaching. Chap, Tubbs, our ranger, and I were hunting bushbuck along a small river with very high banks. About one hundred yards away, three women of different generations were sitting along the river seining for very small fish with nets. They were happily chatting and didn't see us. The ranger suddenly talked to Tubbs and Chap in Ndebele and dashed off into the bush. Chap told me that the ranger was going to arrest the women who, it turned out, were poaching. Strangely, the local indigenous people were not allowed to fish.

We stood on the bank, drawing attention to ourselves. The women undoubtedly wondered what the hell we were doing. Suddenly, the ranger jumped down the bank and apprehended the women. Tubbs and Chap led us back to the truck, where we waited for the ranger and his criminals.

When they arrived at the truck, the ranger took the metal can of three-inch fish and the nets, lined the women up, and began chewing them out, threatening them with prison. The three women hung their heads and didn't reply. When the ranger was finished yelling, he took the seining nets and tore them up. He handed the can of minnows back to them and told them to get lost.

Chap told me that the seine nets were actually mosquito nets, donated by Western anti-malaria charities for the purpose of draping over their beds. The rural Africans saw no value for the actual purpose of the nets, but they made great seining nets. Apparently, the women had a big inventory of nets, so their seining expeditions would continue. Unfortunately, so would malaria.

End of the Hunt

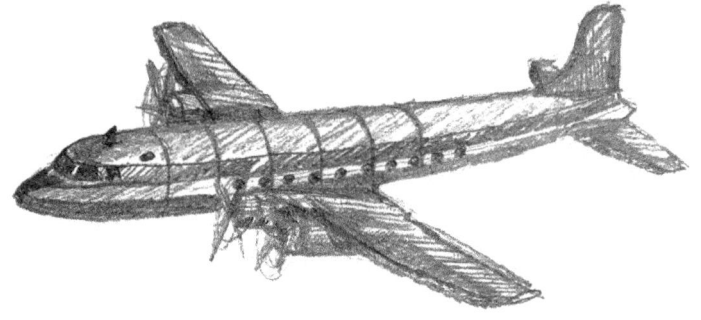

The end of an African hunt can be a depressing time. With each hunt, I had spent a year planning, scheduling, preparing, and anticipating the most incredible adventure of my lifetime. Once there, I walked the wild Africa of Livingstone, Stanley, Burton, Speke, Hemingway, and Rhodes. I had seen lions, elephants, leopards, Cape buffaloes, baboons, and numerous antelope. I'd met strange and wondrous people, including fearless professional hunters and tireless trackers. I'd seen happy Ndebele people bring a bucket of water to their hut once a day and grizzled old white Rhodesians accept the twists and turns of life that societal changes brought upon them.

End of the hunt, overlooking the Ume River

I had my time with them, and I always dreaded it coming to an end.

When I left Africa, I missed many things. I missed having someone beat on my door at five a.m., with me mumbling, "I'm up." I missed groaning as I rolled out of bed, throwing the mosquito netting aside, and reaching for that day's hunting khakis. I missed having the previous day's hunt returning to my mind as I shook away the night's sleep.

I missed the joy of tracking an animal through the African bush and forests, Chap positioning me for a good shot, and then executing it successfully. I missed seeing Chap, Tubbs, and Japhet express their pleasure over the flawless completion of their work, and I missed the wide range of emotions I felt as I walked up to the animal I had just killed.

I missed the disappointing aspects of hunting: not finding tracks, following tracks but not finding the animal, finding the animal but realizing it wasn't what I wanted.

I missed the completion of a day of hard hunting, leaving the camp before dawn and coming back after dusk. Hard hunting is combing the African forests and bush for hours, then tracking an animal for hours. Hard hunting is finding my prey, but choosing to not shoot, and starting over.

I missed staggering into camp at dusk, taking my rifle back to my hut, and dropping my filthy hunting clothes into the hamper for the next day's wash. I missed taking my raggedy, lukewarm shower, climbing into the next day's hunting khakis, heading down to the open dining area, and sitting at the fire pit that overlooked the Ume River. I missed sitting in my chair, as darkness descended, with a Windhoek ale and a basket of fried impala liver, and I missed listening to the whooping hyenas and the moaning lions.

Regardless of the quality of the animals shot, or whether any desired animals were even shot at all, leaving Zimbabwe is always the end of a glorious time. Everything about leaving is sad: waking up the last day, driving to my bush flight to Victoria Falls, flying to Johannesburg—it's all sad. The only part of the journey home that is enjoyable is the time spent in the shops of the O.R. Tambo Airport in Johannesburg, where I am able to buy African souvenirs: stuffed animals for my grandchildren, a dress for my mother, regional hot sauce, jars of salt from the Kalahari Desert, South African hunting magazines, and two-day-old international newspapers.

The flight from South Africa to America allows me to reflect on the time I had in Zimbabwe. After arriving in and then departing from New York, tiredness sets in and culminates with the arrival into Phoenix and the two-hour drive home from the airport.

After taking some time to rest and recover, the sadness fades and is replaced by fervent anticipation as I begin planning the next safari.

Hank's Lion
a short story

Hank tossed and turned, as much as anyone could, in the narrow, first-class seat-becomes-a-bed of the Johannesburg-bound South African Airways flight.

Hank finally gave up. His sleeping pill wasn't working. He glanced at his watch, pressing the stem to illuminate the face. He could read the numbers, 3:16, but he couldn't remember if it indicated New York time, time from takeoff, or the current time in Johannesburg. He groaned and tried to figure out what on earth had prompted him to fly to Zimbabwe to hunt. He didn't even want to hunt. He lowered his head and hoped the pill would kick in. It didn't.

Fifteen hours later, he stepped off the plane at Victoria Falls International into the blinding sunlight of southern Africa. Fumbling with his passport, he elbowed past an elderly couple to get to the head of the customs line. He tossed his passport towards a female customs agent who didn't appreciate his gesture or his attitude. She picked up his passport, opened it, and studied it for ten seconds. She looked up at Hank in utter disdain, and said, "Fifty dollars."

"What for?"

"Entry into Zimbabwe."

"Oh, bullshit."

He dropped his carry-on, pulled out his billfold, and flipped three twenty-dollar bills onto the desk.

The customs agent nodded, stamped his passport, and swept the bills into an open drawer with no intention to make change. She looked up at the irritated passenger dead eyed. Powerless to object, Hank muttered, "Fuck," picked up his carry-on, grabbed his passport, and walked to the baggage pickup room to wait for his suitcase and gun case. When his two luggage pieces slid into the room, Hank picked them up and headed for the arrival hall.

"Sir! Sir!" A uniformed customs agent called after him.

Hank ignored the agent and continued walking. Hank was not interested in dealing with worthless bureaucrats. In midstride, however, two agents stepped on either side of him. Each took an arm. They led him, firmly, into a private room with only a bare table. One of the agents shut the door behind them, then both stood quietly. He looked around and then placed his suitcase on the floor and his rifle case and carry-on on the table.

They all continued to stand; Hank didn't understand what was happening, but he began to realize that he might be in trouble. Several minutes later, two more uniformed customs agents entered the room and walked to the other side of the table from Hank.

"Rifle?" asked one of the agents, pointing to the rifle case.

"Obviously."

"Obvious to whom, if I may ask?"

Hank realized he was annoying the customs agent.

"Yeah, it's my rifle. I'm here to hunt."

"When you return to America, will you have to declare your rifle?"

"Yes. I suppose so." Hank had never flown anywhere with a rifle.

"Well, here too. Do you have your firearm's declaration form?"

Hank wasn't sure what a firearm's declaration form was, but he remembered the forms that his father's secretary had given to him. He pulled some crumpled documents out of his carry-on and thrust them towards the agent.

Smoothing out the firearms forms, the agent said, "Very nice, sir. Thank you. Now, would you take the rifle out of the case?"

After searching his carry-on, he found the key to his rifle case. He opened the case, exposing a brand new, very expensive Wesley Richards .375 H&H bolt-action rifle.

"Sir, would you take the rifle out of the case?"

Hank lifted the rifle from the case and handed it to the agent who read the serial number from the barrel aloud. The other agent verified the number on the declaration form. Hank was surprised when everything matched.

One agent signed all three forms and handed two back to Hank, while the other agent placed the rifle across its case. All four agents left the room, leaving the door open. Irritated by the inconvenience of being challenged by bureaucrats, Hank put the rifle back in the case, threw his carry-on over his shoulder, and walked towards the arrival hall of Victoria Falls International.

As Hank entered the hall, he looked annoyingly across the hustle and bustle. A tall, slender man dressed in khaki shirt and shorts, heavy boots, and a brown, wide-brimmed fedora stepped in front of him. He thrust out his hand. "Hank Lawrence?"

"Uh, yeah. Hi."

"Johan Van Noord. I have the pleasure of being your professional hunter for the next three weeks. Is this your kit?"

Hank was taken aback by the tall man's broad accent. He shook the professional hunter's hand and responded, "Yeah, sure."

Johan took the rifle case from Hank's grasp, grabbed his suitcase, and abruptly made for the exit of the arrival hall. The lanky professional hunter took long, strong strides. Hank was amazed at Johan's seemingly effortless handling of his oversized luggage and rifle case. Still wondering what a kit was, Hank hurried to keep up.

In the airport's small parking lot, Johan slid Hank's baggage into the back of his hunting truck. Turning to Hank, Johan said, "We have a six-hour drive to the hunting camp. I've got cold drinks in the cab. We'll eat if you get hungry."

Hank opened the door on the left side of the truck, threw his carry-on into the back, and climbed in. Strapping on his seat belt, Hank saw things that were different: high-caliber rounds in the cup holder, porcupine quills stuck in the upholstery, strips of tanned skin hanging over the seats, and a large hunting knife stuck between the seats.

"Coke?" Johan offered a can to Hank.

"Yeah. Thanks."

Johan jammed the gear, and they took off down a paved road. Hank noticed things he hadn't seen before: driving on the left side of the road, speed limit signs in kilometers, road signs warning of elephants, and black men and women leading donkey-pulled carts.

"Excited to be here? I have you down for leopard, elephant, and assorted plains game. We should have enough time for some hard elephant hunting."

A frightening image of an elephant charging him ran through Hank's mind. *Elephant? Me? What the hell?*

The whole African safari had been put together by his father and his father's secretary. As Hank's father had told him a few weeks ago, "Just go, Hank. Everything will be arranged for you by Johan. He's a good one. Here is your rifle, ammunition, passport, and entry forms."

"Leopard and elephant?" Hank turned to Johan.

"Yeah. You can knock over an impala for leopard bait. We're already baiting for them along several known leopard trails. Shouldn't be too hard."

Hank turned to look as they sped along the road leading into the Zambezi Valley. *Holy shit*, he thought, *what have I gotten myself into?*

"What do you hunt back in America, Hank? Deer? Elk?"

After a pause, Hank replied, "I've never hunted. I spend all my time managing my family's factories."

Johan glanced at Hank with a surprised look. "Really? Then this should be a great adventure for you."

"Yeah, my dad said I should catch on pretty fast."

Johan paused. "We'll work you into it—sight your rifle, walk after impala, get used to our food. H.L. was right. You'll catch on soon enough."

They came to the end of the paved road. Johan had to cut the truck's speed in half due to the rough, unmaintained dirt roads they were bouncing over.

Wanting to get on an even keel, Johan asked about Hank's father who had hunted with Johan several times. "So, how's old H.L.?" Johan asked cheerfully.

"Don't know. I don't see him that much. I don't want to see him, anyway."

"You don't get along with him?" Johan asked.

"No, I'm a disappointment to him, but I don't care."

Silence.

Johan tried again, "Married? Children?"

"No. Married twice, and they both dumped me after they got their money. Fortunately, I didn't have children with either of those bitches."

Silence.

"Well, Hank, maybe this trip will help you get along with your father."

"Yeah. Maybe."

A greater kudu bull suddenly flashed by the truck. "Look at that, Hank. He's a beauty. I bet we could track one down for you."

Barely seeing the antelope as it flashed by, Hank didn't reply.

"This is beautiful land, Hank. Still primitive. I've been guiding hunters here for twenty years."

For the first time, Hank actually looked at Johan. "How did you start hunting?" he asked.

"My family ran a cattle ranch in the lowveld, the southern part of Zimbabwe," Johan said. "I was walking the hills and shooting impala and zebra before I wore long pants. The government took our ranch, but I didn't want to leave my homeland, so I began guiding hunts. My biggest pleasure is guiding clients on dangerous game hunts like lions, elephants, and leopards. That's when my clients achieve their life goals.

"Most of my clients are aggressive and enthusiastic," he continued. "They're often too aggressive and too enthusiastic, but that's the great aspect of guiding you Americans on these hunts."

Hank looked out the window at the passing African wilderness. The slight shake of his head signaled how terrible he still thought it was that he was here.

They finally arrived at a group of thatched buildings in the middle of the remote African bush, which Johan called the hunting camp. Johan parked on a hard-packed dirt area under the leafy shade of a large tree, which gave relief from the relentless Zimbabwe sun. Two slender black Africans came out from the biggest of the thatched buildings to greet them. One was tall, and the other was short. Both wore torn, faded overalls with "Van Noord Safaris" stenciled on the back. As Hank stepped out of the left side of the truck, the Africans came up to greet him. They both removed their tattered ball caps and stuck out their hands. The taller man introduced himself as Robert, the shorter as Secret. Hank shook their hands but remained silent. Johan rounded the truck and joined the three.

"Secret is my tracker. He'll be guiding us to your animals. Robert here is our mechanic and assistant driver. Johan patted his hunting truck. "He makes sure this old girl gets us there and back," he said.

Johan handed Hank's luggage to Robert and Secret. "Take his kit to Hut Two."

Finally, Hank knew what a "kit" was.

"When you're settled in," Johan continued to Hank, "bring your rifle and a couple rounds to the common room. We'll go down to the riverbed to make sure your scope is squared away."

A half hour later, Hank, with his rifle slung over his shoulder and a pocket full of .375 H&H rounds, walked into the open-air thatched common room that overlooked the Ume River, a seasonally dry, sandy tributary of the Zambezi River. Johan, Secret, and Robert were waiting for him.

"OK. Let's head down to the range." Johan led them down the shallow embankment towards the dry riverbed.

Just yards below the camp, the four men walked up to the hunting sticks: three skinny poles connected at the top and spread to a tripod with a U-shaped rifle holder. Thirty yards away was a cardboard box with a big X painted on the side. The three Zimbabweans stood behind the sticks and waited for Hank to step up with his rifle. Hank hesitated and then looked at Johan.

"Put a couple of rounds into your rifle. Shoot at the X. We can adjust your scope if we need."

Hank fumbled two rounds into the rifle's magazine while the Zimbabweans watched uncomfortably. Finally, he slid the bolt forward and rested his rifle on top of the shooting sticks. Hank aimed towards the box and fired. Sand splashed three yards to the left and well beyond the box.

The Zimbabweans looked at each other.

"Good start," Johan said quietly. "Let's try another."

Hank cranked the bolt and fired, again missing by a significant margin.

"Let's see how your scope is sighted."

Johan stepped forward and took Hank's rifle from him. Hank placed a round into Johan's outstretched palm, who quickly chambered the round and fired. A small circle appeared in the center of the X. Johan looked up from the rifle. "The scope looks okay, Hank. Want to try a few more?"

"No. I'm tired. I'm going to my room to sleep."

Hank abruptly turned and started up the incline with Johan still holding Hank's rifle. Robert and Secret looked at each other.

Secret, who had tracked dangerous game for Hank's father, asked, "That's H.L.'s son?"

Later in the afternoon, Hank walked into the common room. Johan was sitting in a reclining chair overlooking the Ume River and reading a hunting magazine.

"How are you feeling, Hank? Rested?"

"Yeah. I'm okay."

Hank sat in a chair next to Johan and retreated into silence. Johan returned to his magazine. After a few minutes, Johan stood.

"Like a beer, Hank?"

The question seemed to startle Hank from his thoughts. "Uhhh, sure. I'll take one." Hank stood, stretched, and followed Johan to the cooler. Johan opened two Windhoek Lagers and handed one to Hank. They stood at the railing overlooking the sandy riverbed and watched a troop of baboons playing in the distant trees.

Finally, Hank admitted, "About the shooting this afternoon. I know it wasn't very good. I guess I was nervous."

"I understand. All hunters are nervous when they have to shoot in front of their trackers and hunter the first time. What's important is that you know you were nervous. Now you can get through it. You don't want to be nervous when a Cape buffalo charges. We'll go out tomorrow and shoot again. It'll be much better."

Hank nodded and sipped his beer. But he knew the truth.

The following morning, Hank, Johan, Robert, and Secret returned to the shooting range on the riverbed. The box target and shooting sticks were still there. Hank felt as uncomfortable as he did the day before. He loaded his rifle, set it on the sticks, and pulled the trigger, but the results were the same.

Johan moved close to Hank, adjusted one of the sticks, and lowered his head to Hank's ear. "Have you fired this rifle before?"

Hank's head sagged as he mumbled, "No, I got it just before I left."

Johan patted Hank on the back and moved back from him. "Let's have another go, Hank. It's getting better."

Hank went through ten more rounds before he finally hit the box.

Secret and Robert sat watching from the shade almost five yards behind where Hank was shooting. They were very somber.

Later in the day, they drove into the bush, searching for impala herds. Johan pulled his truck into the shade of a copse of trees. Secret and Robert began unloading the lunch gear. When the chairs were in place, Hank sat and opened his soda. Johan cheerfully turned to Hank.

"I've got a good feeling about this afternoon. There are plenty of impala in these parts."

Hank didn't respond. He spooned beans into his mouth.

Johan looked directly at Hank for several seconds. "Hank, do you want to be here? I really don't think you do."

Hank stared into the bush.

"I hate it here," Hank whispered. "I hate my father. I hate Chicago. I don't want to be anywhere."

Johan held his gaze but said nothing.

"I'm here because my father said that I had to grow a set of balls, or he was going to disinherit me."

Johan continued to stare at Hank. "Well, Hank, do you want to hunt?"

Hank returned to looking into the bush.

The next day, Hank followed Johan, who followed Secret, who was following a meandering impala herd. Johan was thinking that if they got close enough to the herd, Hank would have a decent chance to shoot a respectable ram. That would be good.

Secret slowed and then squatted behind dense foliage. He motioned by hand that a good ram impala was in sight. Johan turned to Hank and pointed ahead to where Secret was squatting. Hank just looked at Johan. Johan knelt and looked back to Secret, who continued to stare blankly at Johan. Johan scurried back to Hank.

"Are you okay, Hank? We have a good impala up here."

"Yeah. My father, the great lion hunter, is going to love me bringing back an impala."

"You need to get used to being here, Hank. It takes time to acclimate, both from the stress of the travel and the newness of the hunt. It's hard."

Hank sighed, worked a bullet into the chamber of his rifle, and walked to where Secret was squatting.

Even after they delivered the ram impala to the skinning shed, Hank was more despondent than after his shooting at the range. He fell into a deep, gloomy silence.

The next day they closed in on a small dazzle of zebras. Johan, Secret, and Hank crawled through the brush up a rise. Johan peered over the crest through a thick bush.

Sighting an acceptable stallion, Johan turned to Hank, but Hank was sitting twenty yards behind the crest, staring into the sky. Hank had dropped into a state of inconsolable depression. Johan looked sadly at Hank, and then turned back to watch the stallion.

Suddenly, the five zebras bolted away. Johan instinctively looked for what caused them to run. Two lionesses had just pulled out of their charge. The zebras had escaped, so the big cats laid down and panted heavily.

Johan heard pads rapidly hammering the hard-baked ground behind him. Deep lungs sucked and exhaled. Johan spun around, still on his knees, gripping his heavy .470 nitro express double rifle. He saw a 400-pound lion, the pride lion to the two zebra hunters, charging Hank, who was now standing and staring at the charging lion but not even raising his rifle in an attempt to protect himself.

Johan jerked to his feet, swung his double around, and fired at the lunging lion.

Appendix A

My Opinion: Hunting Ethics

Since the time that pre-humans climbed down from a tree and walked across the savanna, our species have hunted. In early American history, hunting was specifically for food. While most hunting in America is still for food, some hunting is done to harvest trophies. However, I believe the vast majority of hunting in America is without controversy. There is controversy, however, with hunting in Africa.

When I am questioned about the ethics of hunting, it seems that people are offended for one of two reasons: they either have a general objection to killing animals, or they believe that hunting causes a specific animal to become extinct.

I am sympathetic to the first objection. I can understand a person being repulsed by the killing of an animal.

To the second objection, I rely on the science of state fish and game divisions, the US Fish and Wildlife Service (USFW), the Convention on International Trade in Endangered Species (CITES), other Non-Government Organizations (NGOs), and various countries' fish and game divisions. Based on the field work of various government organizations, I trust them to ensure that I endanger no species' existence.

There is another aspect to African hunting, specifically lion hunting, that is neither completely understood nor usually accepted by people who are against hunting. This aspect deals with the role lions play in the lives of the indigenous people of Africa. Lions are disruptive to African villages. The indigenous people often have cattle that are critical to their well-being. Lions will kill and eat their cattle. When that happens, the villagers respond by poisoning the remaining meat in order to kill the lions, as well as all other scavengers: hyena, jackals, leopard, vultures. The indigenous people see no value in lions and would rather have none living wild in Africa.

If the villagers receive monetary compensation for lions hunted by visitors, giving the living lions value, they wouldn't poison lions who kill the occasional cow. The monetary compensation, of course, comes from Western hunters who buy lion tags.

Note that man-eating lions are not included in this calculation. Man-eaters must be found and eliminated immediately.

Through a series of animal counts performed within areas of Zimbabwe and other African countries, a quota is established for each species in each location for each year. If the animal groups determine that an animal is endangered (cheetah or black-faced impala in Zimbabwe), the country's wildlife managing division will not permit hunting them and the US Fish and Wildlife Service will not allow the animal to be imported. If there are ample numbers of a non-endangered species, quotas will be established, and hunting outfits can sell the animals to clients. This governmental regulation of hunting ensures the survival of animal species.

If an animal is endangered, I will not hunt it. Period. Nobody should. However, if an animal is not endangered as a species, and the species is authorized to be hunted, then I have no ethical concerns with hunting that animal.

Appendix B

Elk Hunting in Utah

I began hunting in earnest while living in Utah in the late 1990s. I was very fortunate to meet Tyler Thatcher, a Utah outfitter who took me under his wing. He helped me buy an appropriate elk rifle (.300 Winchester Magnum) and graciously took me into the Uinta Mountains to hunt cow elk. I hunted cow elk for several reasons: there were a lot of them, the tags were amazingly cheap, and the meat was spectacular. Elk steaks and ground elk, which was mixed with ten percent beef to add fat to the very lean elk meat, were my favorites.

Tyler and I went into the high country east of Salt Lake City, which was deep in snow by early November. We would start at the small community of Coalville and then head up into the mountains. To get up into the wilderness, we would take Tyler's snowmobile. The mountains, forests, and vast valleys were absolutely beautiful. They were isolated, very snowy, and very cold. On several occasions, we would inadvertently roll the snowmobile into a deep snow hole and then have to dig it out, an exhausting task.

Several times, we came across a cow moose with a calf. Since moose are exceedingly dangerous animals, we made sure to avoid any confrontation.

I hunted the area for several years and harvested a cow elk each year. Having been taught to field strip an elk by Tyler, we made the carnivores in the Uinta Mountains very happy, leaving large gut piles behind. I kept the liver, of course, which was taken home for consumption, a precursor of my evening snacks in Africa. The dressed cow elk yielded a hundred pounds of excellent, lean meat. My family enjoyed the elk meat so much that year that they have clamored for it every year since my time in Utah.

Having watched me go out with Tyler, my son Michael decided he wanted to hunt. In order to get his hunting license, he had to attend state youth hunting classes, focusing mostly on safety and state hunting laws.

Upon completion, he received his youth hunting license. Tyler took Michael into the Uinta Mountains to hunt mule deer. I tagged along, but I just had foot surgery for fix broken bones, so I limped along, following the hunters as they hiked out of sight.

After several hours of limping over rough ground in the mountains, I heard a shot. Then another. I ran-limped as quickly as I could manage to the sound of rifle fire.

As I stumbled over the top of a saddleback ridge, I saw Michael and Tyler standing over a mule deer. Using his .270 Winchester rifle, Michael had knocked down a young but legal deer. As I stumbled up, Tyler was guiding Michael through the onerous task of field stripping his buck.

Tyler and Michael carried the deer to Tyler's truck. Later in the afternoon, Mike and I took his deer to a butcher, where Mike chose the meat products (sausage, jerky, steak) he wanted.

Eventually, when my family left Utah in the mid-2000s because of job considerations, my elk hunting and Michael's deer hunting came to an end.

Wolf Hunting in Wyoming

In 1995, wolves were reintroduced into Yellowstone National Park. Prior to this, they had been shot out of the American West, but it became clear that wolves were needed to establish the "natural order of life" in Yellowstone. Elk, deer, and moose were ruining Yellowstone due to over-population and overeating the grasses. To solve this, wolves were brought in from Canada to reduce the number of herbivores, which they did.

Over the next twenty years, the wolf population grew, and the wolf packs began existing outside Yellowstone. While hunting is still outlawed in the park, wolves can be legally hunted in the rest of Wyoming, Montana, or Idaho, as long as it is in accordance with the state hunting laws.

I bought an over-the-counter wolf tag, which allowed me to hunt one wolf in the Absaroka Mountain Range, north of the Wind River in central Wyoming. I then hooked up with Wyoming outfitter Blake Chamley.

It was December when we went on the hunt, and it was very cold. We went into the wilderness in Blake's two-person all-terrain vehicle with bulldozer-like, triangular treads that replaced the four wheels. This vehicle could go anywhere: up, down, powder snow, ice, or just bare ground.

We tracked into the mountain range and found a large bluff that overlooked a valley with frozen streams snaking through it. As we sat on the bluff, Blake let loose a terrifying howl. We got an answer in the distance. Two beautiful Wyoming coyotes began loping towards us. If I had been hunting coyotes, I'd have been in seventh heaven.

We went to another area and Blake howled, but no wolves showed. Each time this happened, we'd relocate, but we never had any luck. There was nothing for us except gorgeous terrain and complete isolation.

After several days, we sat in a hole, a flat valley about five acres, surrounded by the vast mountains. This was the type of terrain that the mountain men of the 1830s would spend the winter in because the surrounding mountains protected them from bad weather. Blake set up a predator calling machine, a little device that broadcast the sound of a wounded rabbit every ten minutes and waved a piece of fur back and forth. We sat behind some boulders about forty yards from the fake rabbit, at the edge of the hole. It was freezing. After two hours, I noticed a lurching animal coming towards us about a thousand yards away. I asked Blake, "Is that a bear?"

"No, that's a wolf coming in. Get ready."

Although it was too far away to shoot, I put the wolf in my sights. It was a big, black wolf, and it was lunging through the crusted snow coming towards us. Its lunging gave it a motion that I mistook as a bear's. Blake's binoculars had a ranging capability. He told me to shoot once it got to two hundred yards.

The wolf took another couple of minutes to get to that range, so I just enjoyed watching it as it worked its way closer.

"OK, any time, shoot!" said Blake.

I centered the rifle's crosshairs on the running wolf and shot. The wolf jerked backwards and then began struggling to get up.

"Shoot again," he said.

I shot again. This time, the wolf laid down for good. Whooping with excitement, Blake and I sprinted to the wolf. When we got there, we saw it was a big, black, collared female. The collar was a thick leather strap with a transmitter on it. It was fastened around the she-wolf's neck leaving her ample room to swallow.

Blake and I took the traditional hunting pictures and then prepared to leave.

While I gathered our supplies and brought them to where the wolf lay, Blake began walking a mile out of the hole to retrieve the ATV. Thirty minutes later, Blake returned, and we tied the she-wolf to the ATV and started out of the Absaroka Mountains. When we finally reached the point that we had cellular service, Blake called the Wyoming Fish & Game Department to report the wolf being harvested. Hunted wolf numbers are kept on a day-by-day basis, with outfitters having to call daily to verify that wolves were still available to be hunted. My wolf was the last wolf hunted that year along the Wind River and, coincidentally, the first moving animal that I had ever shot.

Tim and she-wolf

Blake and I took her to the local Wyoming Fish & Game ranger. He wrote up the condition of the wolf and he took the wolf's collar. I asked the ranger about the information gathered by the collar. He referred me to the Wyoming Wolf Manager, who subsequently told me that my wolf had been the alpha-female of two Wyoming wolf packs, which is unusual. In addition, she was eight years old, three years older than the normal life expectancy of a female wolf.

Later, I had another interesting hunting experience in the Wind River Valley. I was hiking up Verna's Canyon east of the town of Dubois with my .243 Winchester, casually hunting coyote. After an hour of walking, I sat on the edge of a small valley cutting higher above the Wind River. I began calling coyote with a perfect howl, similar to Blake's howl, for a couple of minutes, leaning back to wait for the packs of coyote running towards me. Nothing came. I repeated my coyote howl several times, but always, nothing came.

After a while, I decided to call coyotes with a hyena call. Whoooop… Whoooop. I had the same results, no coyote.

As darkness approached, I gave up. I stood, gathered my equipment, turned around, and saw three mountain goats staring at me, only twenty yards away. I froze. After thirty seconds, they casually turned and began walking up the mountain.

I believe the goats wandered down to look at the fool who thought there were hyena in the Wind River Mountains.

Bison Hunting in Colorado

In Utah, there are tags for wild bison that can be drawn. Since it was virtually impossible to be drawn, I never put in for a tag. Instead, I contacted a bison ranch in Colorado which advertised bison hunting in its valley.

I flew into Denver with my .300 Winchester Magnum rifle, rented a car, and drove up to the ranch. I was met by the ranch owner at the gate. We drove to an isolated location where I fired several rounds to ensure that my scope was still sighted correctly.

When I was confident with my rifle, we drove into the wide valley where many bison stood grazing the prairie grass. To my surprise, we drove up to within thirty yards of a male yearling that weighed about one thousand pounds and climbed out of the vehicle. The bison didn't even look towards us. His group of nearby friends didn't pay any attention to us either.

I walked up to within twenty yards of him and put a 200-grain bullet into his shoulder. He dropped to his knees. He was immediately surrounded by ten or fifteen of his friends, who just stood there looking at him. I had intended to fire another round to apply the coup de grâce, but it was impossible to get a clean shot at him. The ranch owner and I just stood there for five minutes until the bison rolled over. His friends gradually wandered away. We went to get a tractor trailer, hoisted him up, and took him to a butcher. Some weeks later, I got 200 pounds of spectacular bison steaks and hamburger.

It's no wonder the damned things almost went extinct. Bison have no survival behavior.

Appendix C

The Thornton Boys

My hunting proclivity is undoubtedly genetic. My mother's family, the Thorntons, had an extensive background in hunting, fishing, and trapping in the wilds of Missouri.

The Thornton family settled in Virginia in the early part of the nineteenth century. At some point in the middle of that century, the Thorntons moved west to Missouri, which, at that time, was the launching point for those settling the American West. It is not known if the family intended to continue west, but Joseph Ross Thornton, my great-grandfather, settled east of Independence, where he farmed and rode the Baptist Church's traveling pastoral circuit. His son, Silas Ross Thornton, moved west into Independence, where he married my grandmother, Elva Graves, in 1917. My mother, Betty Good née Thornton, was the only daughter of Silas and Elva. Silas's sons—Sidney, Jack, and Ed—grew to become outdoorsmen: hunters, fishers, and trappers.

Back: Sidney, Ed, Jack
Front: rat terrier Cactus, Betty, Elva, Silas

The Thorntons, as many American families, were hit hard by the Great Depression of the thirties. The family lived on hunted game (rabbits, muskrats, and deer), as well as Silas's salary at the Kansas City trolley barn. Eventually, all three boys joined the Civilian Conservation Corps (CCC), a federal work relief program that operated from 1933 through 1942 for unemployed, unmarried men from the ages of seventeen through twenty-eight. Sidney worked with the CCC in California, while Jack was in Nevada, and Ed was in Idaho. Later, Ed took his family to Idaho to visit his working locations, but the structures were worn away by the sixties.

Unknown friend, Ed, Jack, and Sidney with rabbits

Uncle Sidney, the oldest of the boys, served in the US Army in World War II. He was with General Patton in Europe and was with the units who discovered the infamous concentration camps in Germany. He stayed in Germany for a few years after the war, meeting and marrying his German wife Margaret. They had a son, Austin, who served in the US Army, and eventually disappeared from the family.

Sidney was a noted outdoorsman in central and western Missouri. My cousin Jack, Uncle Jack's son, showed me a 1950s newspaper clipping of a huge sixty-five-pound beaver Sidney trapped near Independence.

Uncle Jack, the middle boy, became a World War II B-24 pilot and subsequent prisoner of war in Germany. After the war, Jack married my mother's best friend, Joyce, and had two children, Jack and Gwynn. He stayed in the US Air Force after the war and eventually retired in the 1960s. He became a high school teacher, and later a counselor, in Missouri, and often took my brother and me trapping in the cold Missouri autumns. We once trapped a muskrat, which Uncle Jack skinned, tanned its fur, and sold it for one dollar.

Uncle Eddie, the youngest of the boys, served in the US Coast Guard during World War II. Later in life, Ed took his wife, Jean, and children, Dennis and Janice, on extensive driving vacations into the Rockies. Ed loved to fish for trout in the cold, clear streams that fell down from the mountains of Colorado. Closer to home, Eddie fished the Sac River and the Osage River in southwest Missouri with Dennis and others in the Thornton family.

Silas and Elva had a cabin on Soap Creek near Gravois Mills at the Lake of the Ozarks in the late forties and early fifties. The Thornton family, including my parents, brother, and me, would gather there to explore the woods for the Three Bear's Cabin, seine Soap Creek for fish, chase rabbits, watch for rattlesnakes, and generally enjoy the Lake community.

Like many families, the Thorntons have numerous myths developed throughout the ages. These are some of my favorites:

> Purportedly, my great-grandmother Minnie Grace was a full-blooded Cherokee. She fell in love with Joseph Thornton. Naturally, a Baptist minister couldn't possibly marry a Native American woman, so great-grandma Minnie Grace told everybody she was French. It worked. Nobody believed she was Cherokee. Later, in the sixties, Uncle Jack went to Oklahoma trying to document the Thornton association with the Cherokee Nation. He was unable. I attempted to have my mother DNA tested to show our blood association with the Cherokee Nation. For reasons that my daughter patiently explained to me, it wasn't possible.

> Apparently, Silas was acquainted with Frank James, older brother of Jessie and leader of the James Gang, ruffians in the 1860s and 1870s. When Jessie was killed by the "dirty little coward" Bob Ford in 1882, Frank surrendered to the governor

of Missouri and left the life of crime. Sidney, as a child, learned that Silas would meet with Frank. Sidney asked if Silas was frightened by the notorious bad man. Silas answered, "No, son, he was just an old fat man." I've visited Frank's grave in Independence several times, reminiscing about this story.

Silas was an avid sportsman and athlete. He played semi-pro baseball into his forties as a catcher. He coached local basketball and frequently took public transportation to Lawrence, Kansas to watch the University of Kansas Jayhawks play basketball.

During the depression, Silas sustenance fished. His fishing wasn't sport; it was to feed his family, so it was of critical importance that he brought home fish. Did he use fancy fly fishing gear or costly lures? Nope. When fishing out of town, he used dynamite, illegal even in the wilds of Missouri. He would light the fuse and drop the stick into the water. When the dynamite went off, there was a muffled whoop, followed by a rolling of the water. Fish would then float to the surface, at which point he could gather his bounty.

Whenever I think of the Thornton Boys, I think of rugged American outdoorsmen. In an earlier time, the Thornton Boys would have been the first over the Cumberland Gap, or the first to see the Rocky Mountains, or the first to see the Pacific Ocean. They were adventurers caught in a settled time.

www.ingramcontent.com/pod-product-compliance
Lightning Source LLC
Chambersburg PA
CBHW040802150426
42811CB00081B/2372/J